Making
PASSWORDS
SECURE

Making PASSWORDS SECURE

Fixing the weakest link in cybersecurity

DOVELL BONNETT

Library of Congress Cataloging-in-Publication Data
Bonnett, Dovell
Making Passwords Secure: Fixing the Weakest Link in Cybersecurity

ISBN: 978-1530164486

Cover Design: Fiona Jayde
Interior Design: Tamara Cribley

www.Access-Smart.com

1. Computers & Technology. 2. Security & Encryption. 3. Network Security.

To my beautiful, loving and supportive wife, Marguerite.
Without your support and encouragement, this book would not have been possible.

And to every business owner, IT manager, and employee
who experiences password fatigue.

DISCLAIMER

Because of the dynamic nature of the Internet, any Web addresses or links contained in this book may have changed since publication and may no longer be valid. The views expressed in this work are solely those of the author and do not necessarily reflect the views of the publisher, and the publisher hereby disclaims any responsibility for them.

The author of this book does not dispense legal advice or prescribe the use of any technology as a form of absolute protection from hackers. The intent of the author is only to offer information of a general nature to help you in your quest for computer security. In the event you use any of the information in this book for yourself, or your company, which is your constitutional right, the author and the publisher assume no responsibility for your actions.

PRAISE FOR *MAKING PASSWORDS SECURE*

I most highly recommend reading the timely and informative book by Dovell Bonnett, "Making Passwords Secure: Fixing the Weakest Link in Cybersecurity". As companies, individuals are increasingly being subjected to breaches and ransomware attacks, the need for cybersecurity awareness and safeguards have become paramount. Thankfully, Dovell, who has been creating computer security solutions for over 20 years, offers a one-stop guide book on how to mitigate cyber threats by explaining the basis and tactics of authentication security. The book is written in a concise style that provides useful information for both laymen and serious techies. It is a book that should be on everyone's reading list!

~ Chuck Brooks, Vice President, Sutherland Government Solutions

If you want to find out about the world of multi-factor authentication in a less technical and more informative way, I can genuinely recommend this book.

~ Sandra Jones, Principal, Sandra Jones and Company

Addictive... Introduces readers to this brave new world of technology, where hackers roam free, and victims include nearly anyone on the Web. Dovell presents this myriad of cyber weaknesses and attack examples in a matter-of-fact voice with intriguing real world examples throughout. It's both fun and informative.

~Eileen Kent, The Federal Sales Sherpa, President, Custom Keynotes, LLC

Understanding the weak points in cybersecurity allows IT to fill them, but not without a budget. CEOs need to understand what their CISOs are facing. No one points this out better than Dovell. Logging on to your computer network will have a new meaning after reading this book.

~Sherman Crancer, Microsoft PCDM

Dovell Bonnett urges business owners to take responsibility for their computer networks and cybersecurity. If you don't get your employees out of the position of network security administrator, then the responsibility of a data breach will be on the owners.

~ William Yeadon, CEO, Chase Security Solutions, Australia

This book is a MUST-READ for any manager in the IT industry. While there are many, competing priorities in information technology, being conversant on the notion of a "Password Authentication Infrastructure" is critical enough to demand everyone's attention. I have received so many "ah-ha" moments as I read this book; things that are right before my eyes that I have given little thought or to which I have paid little attention. Thank you Dovell for opening my eyes to the one commonly used, yet overlooked security vulnerability! Thank you for providing a road-map to addressing this is an effective way! Your writing style and appropriate humor made this topic very digestible!

~ Karen Clay, IT Director, Carlos Rosario International Public Charter School

Making Passwords Secure is a must-read for everyone. No matter what business you're in, strong passwords and effective password management are critical for maintaining secure networks. Dovell Bonnett has done us all a favor by combining his knowledge, helpful stories, and extensive research in an easy-to-read format. Get this on your bookshelf today!

~ Dietrich Wecker, Security Software Developer

Multi-factor authentication is essential for good security, with a remembered password as a common factor. Dovell Bonnett writes in a clear, easy-to-understand, non-technical style, with useful information. This book claims to be "A guide to understanding the weakest links, and appropriate solutions for cybersecurity." I feel it meets these claims, and more.

~ Hitoshi Kokumai, President, Mnemonic Security, Inc.

In this thought-provoking work, Dovell Bonnett digs into the nuts-and-bolts of the authentication challenge and talks about why username-and-password isn't going away anytime soon but can be made secure for many applications. As "The Password Guy," Dovell debunks many of the myths of infallibility surrounding multi factor authentication and other high-technology solutions, in favor of a pragmatic approach to password management that is a 99% solution to this often vexing enterprise challenge.

~Chris Williams, co-author of *Enterprise Cybersecurity: How to Build a Successful Cybersecurity Program Against Advanced Threats*

ACKNOWLEDGEMENTS

I want to thank the many people who have helped make this book and my business possible. First and foremost, I want to acknowledge Dietrich and Christine Wecker, and Marc Jacquinot for their friendship and collaboration. They ignited my passion for secure password authentication and supported my mission to make ID badges "do more than make a door go beep."

I also want to thank those people who, over my 25 years in the industry, have contributed to my knowledge and understanding of smartcards, cryptography, and the business ramifications of technology. Thank you, John Corbett, Jody Zimmerman, Juergen Hammerschmitt, Chris Goeltner, Robert Merkert, Steve Hamilton, Anne Gregory, Bob Gilson, Alex Giakoumis, Shirley Gonzalez, Mark McGovern, Bryan Ichikawa, Bruce Ross, Mike Dusche, Mark Scaparro, and Dominic Piperno for sharing your time, knowledge, and insight.

I also want to thank the many people within the Microsoft community who encouraged me to write this book. I first need to recognize Casey Watson who had to put up with my badgering question, "So how do you log into Azure?" I also want to thank Sherman Crancer, Candy Stark, Justin Slagle, Maryam Al-Hammami, Kimberley Kenner, Jonathan Frieber, Lacy Finley, David Gersten, Dave Seibert, Veronica Place, Bill Hole, Eric Klauss, and all the other wonderful members of IAMCP. These people and many more who I am just getting to know are amazing, and it is my privilege to know them.

Finally, there are individuals whose guidance and insight have contributed to my business growth and professionalism who I also want to thank: Michael Jalaty, Diane Kehlenbeck, Eileen Kent, Chuck Brooks, Terry Gold, Chris Williams, Hitishi Kokumai, Tamara Bill, Denise Griffitts, Martin Kleckner, Dane Kinnear, Donald Kasle, Denzil Barber, Karen Clay, Mike Rudderow, Aaron Flick, Keith Cunningham, Tom Hope, and Dr. Neil Kalin.

I have been incredibly lucky to have so many people help me throughout my career. It would be impossible to thank them all. I offer this book in gratitude to them all, with my promise to pay it forward.

TABLE OF CONTENTS

I BELIEVE...

...that an individual's personal information should ideally remain in their possession. When your identity is handed over to or managed by a third party, you can lose both your identity and your security.

Identity has become the technology that interfaces with digital devices, software, and the Internet. Technology has been changing and directing how we operate in the world for as long as it has been in existence. It's time to turn the tide and begin directing technology to operate in ways that work for individuals. Humans should be telling digital devices not just what we want them to do, but also how we want them to do it, not the other way around.

Secure authentication is no exception. Instead of being a slave to passwords and the technologies that require them, let me show you how to make technology bend to your will by *Making Passwords Secure.*

Dovell Bonnett
Founder and CEO of Access Smart

INTRODUCTION

The information in this book is a game changer for both business people and technical people. Business owners, corporate officers, agency managers, and financial decision makers will gain a high-level understanding about what the IT administrator or Chief Information and Security Officer (CISO) worries about and needs in order to protect the business.

The CISO, IT Administrator, and other technology recommenders will gain a greater appreciation for what the business side must have to create purchasing approvals and be better able to communicate what they need, without bogging the business folks down with tech speak.

By arming you with targeted information to make informed decisions about cybersecurity technology, this book is designed to help you implement the best security solution for your organization, become a hero in the boardroom, and protect against a security breach that would seriously damage your company.

It is essential for everyone to understand the one link in your company's computer security chain that is the most ignored and overlooked hole in cybersecurity:

User Authentication and the Management of Passwords.

There are those in the computer security industry who claim that passwords are dead. They are wrong. You'll learn why in Chapter 1. There are those who believe passwords are insecure. They, too, are wrong. That's in Chapter 2. There are those who claim that certificate-based authentication is super-secure and is the only way to protect data. They are only partially correct because certificates are not as strong as they would like you to believe. That's in Chapters 3 and 7. In Chapters 4 and 5, you will learn how many companies, even ones with extensive backend security, could be leaving their virtual front door unlocked. And if anyone ever tries to convince you there is no way to calculate cybersecurity's Return On Investment, have them read Chapter 9. Finally, Chapter 10 will give you a step-by-step plan to implement the right cybersecurity infrastructure for your situation. These are just a few reasons to read this book.

The many mistaken and incomplete understandings about cybersecurity that are commonplace today drove me to write this book. The truth in this book may not set you free, but it will save you time, money, and valuable resources.

In November 2014, I was invited by a very large computer software company to learn about their newest product and the latest security features they had implemented to protect their customers' information. While the presenter spoke, I sat quietly listening and nodding, but expressing no excitement or praise for what they were conveying. Afterward, the presenter came over to me and asked me point-blank if I was impressed with what they had done. I told him I was impressed, but I had one simple question. The conversation went something like this:

Dovell: "How do you log in to your software?"

Presenter: With a confused, but also 'you're an idiot' look on his face, he said, "With your computer."

Dovell: "Yes, I understand. But how do you log in to your software?"

Presenter: In a perturbed voice, he said, "With your user account information."

Dovell: "Right. That's great. But how do you log in to the software?"

Presenter: Now, in a tone of almost pure disgust and a 'Why am I wasting my time with you' attitude, he said, "With your user name and password."

Dovell: "Exactly! And as soon as my password is stolen, all that amazing backend security no longer matters."

That was the moment when he finally understood the importance of secure authentication. The software was Microsoft's Azure. After that meeting, I worked with Microsoft to put out a press release announcing how Power LogOn® and Azure together secures your data from fingertips to storage.

Cybersecurity needs to start when the computer is first turned on. If just anyone can turn on your computer, all security bets are off. If you wait until the user is past the firewall to authenticate him, you are too late.

As the owner, manager, or chief officer of a business or agency, you are responsible for funding cybersecurity investments. If you don't understand what you are buying and why you need it (or don't need it,) then how can you know if you are making the right choices?

According to the National Cyber Security Alliance, forty percent of small- to medium-size businesses are victims of a cyber breach. Sixty percent of those SMBs go out of business within six months. And while large enterprises may be able to weather an attack, they will spend hundreds of thousands to millions of dollars in damage control and trying to shore up their computer networks. Even then, money cannot solve all the issues of a successful data breach.

No matter what size business or agency you are dealing with, this book will lead you step by step along a path to protect your data, your company, and yourself by understanding and building secure, trusted identity authentication. That trust begins by first... **Making Passwords Secure.**

CHAPTER 1

THE REAL PROBLEM
WITH PASSWORDS

"I am concerned for the security of our great Nation; not so much because of any threat from without, but because of the insidious forces working from within."

~ General Douglas MacArthur

Today's computer networks are complex and decentralized, creating multiple points for hackers to attack. This fact alone makes cybersecurity both important and difficult for information technology (IT) administrators to achieve. These managers not only have to deal with keeping servers, operating systems and applications up-to-date, but now they are also tasked with managing Bring Your Own Devices (BYOD), Clouds, phishing, pharming, social engineering, and many other threats.

Because we live in the Internet age, IT managers also worry about the network security of other companies, something they have zero control over. Sending a simple email from one person to another may involve hundreds of vulnerabilities.

Despite all these attack points, whenever a data breach is reported in the news, the lack of strong passwords often gets blamed first. The main reason passwords are the easy scapegoat (especially in the media) is because people actually know what passwords are and everyone is frustrated with trying to manage them.

Password authentication is not the problem.

The *management* of passwords is the
real security nightmare.

In our world of ever-increasing cyber-attacks, IT invests massive amounts of time, resources, and money to secure corporate networks and data, train employees to be wary of attacks, and perform 24/7 monitoring of data traffic to spot anomalies. Because there are no silver bullets, many different security technologies are utilized to address each potential threat, and often not in a coordinated fashion.

With so many vulnerability points for hackers to target, where should cyber-security start? The first line of defense must be **trusted authentication of the user.** User authentication has to start when you turn on the computer, *before* the operating system is fully loaded. If authentication takes place behind the firewall, where Single Sign-On and One-Time Password technologies reside, it's too late. For the vast majority of computers in the world today, an end-user implements authentication via a user name and password. That makes password authentication the elephant in the room everyone is ignoring.

There are three considerations when evaluating the security of passwords:

1. Password Authentication;
2. Password Management; and
3. Password Infrastructure.

When these three considerations are successfully integrated, making passwords secure is not only possible, but passwords actually become a very effective, cost-efficient, and user-friendly feature contributing to robust cybersecurity.

Password Authentication is Secure!
Password Management is the Beast!

IT managers, along with a multitude of costly network security protections, frequently cannot prevent a breach because a legitimate user name and password is used. How do hackers and criminals acquire legit user names and passwords? The easiest targets are employees.

The ten most common criticisms levied against passwords include:

1. Passwords are not long enough to be secure
2. Passwords don't always include different cases, numbers, and special characters
3. Passwords use words that can be found in a dictionary
4. Users choose passwords that include personal information
5. The same password is used on multiple sites
6. Passwords are not changed frequently
7. Users write passwords on notes or store them in smartphones, computer files, etc.
8. People can look over your shoulder as you type passwords
9. Malware programs like keyloggers capture passwords as a user types them
10. Users disclose passwords to hackers through social engineering tricks

Think about it. Are these complaints the fault of password authentication viability, or how and who manages those passwords? It makes no difference what authentication method you use, including certificates and biometrics (the ability to use anatomical, physiological, or behavioral characteristics as unique identifiers). If the authentication methodology can be compromised, the system will be breached.

Where passwords were used to gain unauthorized access, investigators eventually discovered that hackers simply took advantage of poor password management or social engineering tactics. These breaches had nothing to do with whether passwords are a secure and viable means of authentication. When corporations task their employees with managing their own passwords, they inadvertently put the most insecure element of security in charge of security. Since no manager wants to blame his/her employees, passwords take the hit.

This is not to say that employees are bad people or are out to defeat cybersecurity. Far from it. Because of staffing cutbacks, most employees today are working harder than ever. They have more responsibilities and more stress than ever before. Managing the average 50 to 100 user names and passwords while trying to follow complex password policies can become so cumbersome that employees look for shortcuts to create what they see as efficiencies. Unfortunately, those shortcuts can wreak havoc on a company by creating vulnerabilities that thieves exploit to steal customer credit card information, customer passwords, company confidential data, and more. All you have to do is listen to the news reports after a data breach to hear the horrors. Many of those could have been prevented by incorporating a robust enterprise password manager that takes the employee out of the business of securing the network.

Passwords Are Not Going Away Anytime Soon

Computer authentication is made up of three parts (called "factors"): something you Have, something you Know, and something you Are. Together, the industry refers to these as "the three factors of authentication."

Passwords are the something you *know*. If passwords disappeared completely, then authentication would be left with only two factors. This is something no security professional would ever support. Finally, passwords are the only factor of the three that can be easily, cheaply, and frequently changed. That's why, as an authentication methodology, passwords are both effective and here to stay.

> **Note:** A new authentication factor is under discussion since the introduction of GPS-enabled smartphones. The new proposed factor is "Where you Are."

What *Needs* to be Fixed is How Users Manage Passwords

Employees (or end-users) are the weakest link in any computer network for three reasons. First, they do a very poor job of generating passwords. The passwords they choose are easy to crack. Second, they can't remember their passwords, so they write them down and store them in places where they (and others) can find them. And third, end-users are susceptible to social engineering schemes (aka human hacking) which hackers use to get people to voluntarily give up their passwords.

> When employees are given the responsibility to generate, know, remember, type, and manage passwords, IT has inadvertently given employees the job title "Network Security Manager."

⚏ SOMETHING TO THINK ABOUT

You may remember the movie "Catch Me If You Can" staring Leonardo DiCaprio, Tom Hanks, and Christopher Walken. The movie was about

Frank Abagnale, who in 1963 started as a con artist (social engineer.) Fast-forward to the computer age where the poster kid for computer social engineering has to be Kevin Mitnick. Kevin was a hacker and fugitive, breaking into computer networks, creating false identities, and running from authorities for years. At one point when the FBI was closing in to arrest Kevin, he escaped, but not before leaving a fresh box of donuts in the refrigerator marked "FBI donuts."

In his book *The Art of Deception*, Kevin shares how he used social engineering, not hacking tools, to discover passwords so he could break into computers. Kevin also says, "Testifying before Congress not too long ago, I explained that I could often get passwords and other pieces of sensitive information from companies by pretending to be someone else and just asking for it." He goes on to explain that social engineering takes advantage of people's gullibility, naiveté, ignorance, and stupidity. A quote from Albert Einstein sums up Kevin's philosophy: "Only two things are infinite, the universe and human stupidity, and I'm not sure about the former."

Like Frank Abagnale, Kevin was eventually caught, served his time and now runs a computer security consulting firm where he helps businesses secure their computer networks. I'm sure Kevin would agree that one of the best ways to prevent data breaches is to get the employee out of the role of network security manager!

Myth: Users Must Know Their Passwords

The concept of a password or pass phrase dates back to ancient times. They were required for access into places like a castle, camp or even a professional guild, such as the Freemasons Society. A guardian would challenge the visitor for the password. If the stranger answered correctly, he was recognized as a friend and allowed to pass. If the wrong password was used, swords were drawn.

During World War II, Americans used passwords like "Lollypop," "Licorice," or "Lollapalooza" because the Japanese language does not have the "L" sound, which made it difficult for Japanese soldiers to pronounce these words.

In modern times, computer passwords have become the digital authentication representing the "something you know." Where and how a person reveals their password has changed significantly (from a sentry to a computer) and it's time for an update to our understanding of how passwords should and can function in the twenty-first century.

The current definition of "password" according to Dictionary.com is:

Password: noun

1. A secret word or expression used by authorized persons to prove their right to access, information, etc.

2. A word or other string of characters, sometimes kept secret or confidential, that must be supplied by a user in order to gain full or partial access to a multiuser computer system or its data resources.

One of the biggest misconceptions about passwords is that passwords must be the thing that a <u>person</u> *knows, types, or speaks.* That is literally an ancient and false belief! In the wake of massive computer advancements, why are humans still being asked to generate, know, and reveal passwords? Shouldn't technology be doing that?

Here's my take on an updated definition of "password:"

Password: noun

1. A shared secret expression or other string of characters exchanged human-to-human, human-to-computer, or computer-to-computer for the purpose of authenticating access to facilities, services, computer networks, and/or data.

Not only does a user *not* need to know his password, he also *shouldn't* have to remember it or type it. This is good for both the end-user and network security because it diminishes the effectiveness of social engineering hacks. How can an employee reveal something he doesn't even know?

Hackers vs. Crackers

The media has confused hackers and crackers. Not all hackers are crackers, but all crackers are hackers.

A hacker (also called a White Hat hacker) is someone who is able to analyze, take apart, and then re-assemble a device or code to make it do something it was never intended to do.

A cracker (also known as a Black Hat hacker) is an individual with the same skills as a hacker, but they use their knowledge to do harm for personal or financial gain. The harm or devastation they do to businesses, governments, and individuals is of no concern to them. In this book, when I use the word "hacker," I am referring to that person's ability to break a system. However, when the break is used for illegal or malicious purposes, I use the term "cracker."

Identity Theft

The theft of an individual's computer credentials is fast outpacing the theft of credit card data. Credentials allow unfettered access to accounts and services. With the identity theft epidemic, how can one really be sure that a person is who they say they are?

Driver's licenses can easily be forged, Social Security numbers stolen, and fake passports printed, resulting in trusted documents being brought into question. Legitimate and honest registration authorities and certificate authorities are having a difficult task trusting the documentation and identity of individuals requesting certificates. Fraudulent documents lead to fraudulent certificates, which lead to serious cyber-attacks and data breaches.

Identity theft is much more than a stolen credit card. Many laws require companies to report breaches, and the penalties are far more severe for the business than they are for the criminals utilizing the false identity. Additionally, there are very few laws to help victims and make the recovery process manageable. The number one way individuals are exposed to identity theft is through corporate data breaches, making this a massive problem.

Companies need to understand both the direct and indirect costs of a data breach. While different organizations calculate the costs in different ways, the Ponemon Institute is the most widely quoted research firm that analyses the costs of a data breach to companies. According to Ponemon's *2015 Cost of Data Breach Study* report, the average cost to a company *per sensitive record* lost or stolen in the United States over the last few years is:

- **2013:** $188 per record for a combined average total cost of $5.40M per company

- **2014:** $201 per record for a combined average total cost of $5.85M per company

- **2015:** $217 per record for a combined average total cost of $6.53M per company

Defending against data breaches and identity theft is outside the scope of this book. There are books on the market that address that topic specifically. From my perspective, data security must start before the firewall when a computer is first turned on. Having a strong, secure Password Authentication Infrastructure (PAI) is a key component to safeguarding computer networks.

Chain of Trust

A chain of trust is built on the premise that within a computer network, all hardware and software is authorized and disperses information only to authorized users or places. The problem with networks today is that they are so complex and decentralized. One weak link within this chain becomes a portal hackers can exploit to gain access to other parts of the network, until they eventually achieve full system administrative rights. Then, all confidential data and private information becomes available for the hackers to use as they wish.

Crackers are highly motivated to access private information for their own personal, financial, political, or social gain. And they have a vast arsenal at their disposal to penetrate a network: technology, social engineering, careless employees, indirect network connections, and more.

The best IT can do is to try to protect against <u>known</u> attacks, which is an almost futile endeavor. Trying to protect against every known attack is not only cost prohibitive, but hackers and crackers constantly make minor modifications to their attacks in their efforts to get past security. They have copies of every antivirus software on which they test their malware over and over, tweaking it until it gets through. Then they release it before anyone has a defense. This fact alone gives crackers a huge advantage. It also creates the greatest fear of the Chief Information Officer (CIO) and Chief Information Security Officer (CISO): the <u>unknown</u> attacks.

When a hacker decides to break into a network, what do you think he wants most? What does he go after first? Ideally, he wants the network administrator's authentication credentials because he knows that will give him complete access. He starts wherever he sees the weakest link, using that point to burrow his way in. Once he gets the desired credentials, he has free rein of the entire network to access confidential data, inject malware, or reprogram peripheral hardware to perform unintended tasks.

⊞ SOMETHING TO THINK ABOUT

I recently heard a White Hat hacker tell a shocking story. A bank hired him to test their network. In a matter of minutes, he was in their network snooping around. That was his first task. While in the network, he came across some IP addresses that he didn't recognize. After a quick investigation, he discovered they were the IP addresses for the bank's network of ATMs. Wanting to test the security of the ATMs, he wrote and uploaded a program into the network to have a specific ATM spit out a twenty-dollar bill the next day at 12:02 a.m. At the appointed hour, he hopped in his car and drove to the remote location. Just before midnight, he set up a video camera and pointed it at the dark ATM machine. He waved at the camera and waited. At 12:02 a.m., right on schedule, the ATM magically came to life. The screen lit up, the cash door opened, and the machine spit out a twenty-dollar bill.

It doesn't matter how or where a breach occurs, once the hacker has broken in, the entire network loses the chain of trust.

Password Alternatives

The plethora of computer breaches and password database thefts has caused some security pundits to rail against passwords. Michael Daniel, Special Assistant to President Obama and the U.S. Cybersecurity Coordinator (Cyber Czar), said recently, "One of my key goals in my job that I would really love to be able to do is to kill the password dead." But, what would replace passwords? Certificates? Biometrics? Smartphones? Or something else?

A digital "certificate" is the combination of cryptographic functions (symmetric and asymmetric ciphers, hashing, and digital signature) with infrastructure components (Registration and Certificate Authorities, encryption acceleration hardware, Key management, HSM, and smartcards) used to generate an electronic "passport." This passport or certificate allows individuals, computers, and organizations to trust each other over the networks and to securely exchange information.

Certificate authentication, which can be expensive and is not necessary for every business environment, offers high levels of assurances that the identity of a person or device really is who they say they are. However, there are many cases where sloppy identity authentication, poorly managed keys, and the subpoenas of Private Keys make certificate-based systems just as weak and vulnerable as poorly managed password systems. Because of the overall infrastructure complexity of certificate-based systems and the false sense of security some IT managers place in digital certificates, they can be more vulnerable to an attack than some security experts are willing to acknowledge.

Biometrics also have cost and implementation considerations. And smartphones require charging and monthly service fees. All these alternatives do have a place in specific environments, but they cannot replace the humble password across the board.

That is why I am introducing a new concept I call "**Password Authentication Infrastructure**" (PAI.) Like all security infrastructures, PAI is based on combining and utilizing the strengths of many different technologies and techniques which, when taken together, become stronger than their parts.

Password Authentication Infrastructure (PAI) for enterprise networks addresses four basic principles:

1. Removal of the user as a network security manager
2. Creation of IT centrally managed secure passwords and policies
3. Installation of a strong password manager
4. Utilization of multi-factor authentication

> When cracking passwords becomes as difficult as cracking cipher keys, then passwords will be secure.

This book does *not* compare the operational functions or benefits of ciphers versus passwords, because they are unrelated. Ciphers are software algorithms used to encrypt data. Passwords are a means of user authentication.

This book *does* analyze an important cipher component that the security industry goes to great lengths to protect: the keys. Keys are the secrets you need to know to unlock the cipher algorithm. If a Key is ever compromised, it will not matter how great an algorithm is because it will have been made instantly worthless. In my opinion, cipher keys are really just glorified passwords. In fact, the only thing distinguishing keys from passwords is that far more time and money is spent securing keys, while password protection is often ignored.

> When security is cumbersome to use, end-users will circumvent security for convenience. But, convenience without security is neither convenient nor secure.

Password security is easy to fix and far more economical to implement than a cumbersome and complex Public Key Infrastructure (PKI). I admit, there are environments where PKI is appropriate, but it is not an efficient or appropriate use of resources for most companies. The good news is, there are other choices along the computer security spectrum between simple user-managed passwords and PKI.

At the opposite end of the spectrum from PKI, simple password managers may be convenient, yet how they are implemented can be anything but secure. Using an Internet browser to secure passwords is extremely insecure because anyone using that computer can access them. Companies like Trend Micro, Google, and LastPass have all experienced security breaches. Password security involves so much more than just a password manager. Robust password security requires an infrastructure.

In this book, you will discover exactly how symmetric and asymmetric keys are similar to passwords, what makes these encryption key methodologies appropriate for select environments, and how the same security techniques can be deployed to protect passwords for everyone else. A Password Authentication Infrastructure (PAI) can drastically improve a company's return on investment (ROI). And yes, it really is possible to make employees, executives and IT professionals happy, secure, and productive.

It's time to tame the password beast!

CHAPTER 2

THE CURRENT STATE OF PASSWORDS

"Our problems stem from our acceptance of this filthy, rotten system."

~ Dorothy Day, American Journalist

Password data looms as a primary target for nefarious crackers because it is the easiest way to gain access into a company's network. Just because data are stolen does not mean it has been used to commit a fraud. Fraud begins when criminals exploit stolen credentials to gain unauthorized network access.

In my first book, *Online Identity Theft Protection for Dummies®*, I explained the difference between "identity theft" and "identity fraud." The same holds true for password theft vs. password fraud:

Password data *theft* is the actual stealing of passwords through data breaches, social engineering, and a multitude of other means.

Password authentication *fraud* is the act of using someone else's identity to gain unauthorized access into a computer network.

Securing a company against theft involves different protocols than securing against fraud. Password Authentication Infrastructure (PAI) addresses both.

IT first needs the tools to safeguard password data. If password data becomes compromised, IT should have the capability of making it all useless. Second, the system needs to be able to authenticate that the real authorized user is actually presenting the password entered. This is where multi-factor authentication comes in.

Who Should Manage the Password?

IT can inadvertently be its own worst enemy when it comes to security. Employees often see security policies as a hindrance to their jobs, which forces them to circumvent security for their own personal convenience. In my experience, IT appears to overlook this fact.

I talk to many Chief Information Security Officers (CISOs) and I always ask them if they have a secure log-on policy. They all give me the same resounding "Yes!" According to these CISOs, they have implemented a password policy made up of the same old requirements we've been hearing about since the 1990s: use eight to nine characters, different character types, change them every sixty to ninety days, and do not allow the reuse of the last five passwords. When I ask those same CISOs *how* the employees *manage* their policy, they have no idea. Their only concern seems to be that they have a "strong" policy in place.

The Weakest Link

What IT is missing is that network security is only as strong as its weakest link. They themselves put the weakest link—the user—in charge of implementing IT's policies. Employees tend to create shortcuts and workarounds that include using the same password in multiple places, writing them down, or trying to come up with something that is easy to remember and type. This combination of security policies and users' habits is what makes computer networks inherently insecure. My concern is that these CISOs are thinking only from the perspective of their side of the security fence, about meeting security compliance requirements, and not about how the employee/end-user is going to manage those policies. The implementation (not the existence) of strong policies determines a company's network vulnerability.

Today, the average number of accounts that each user has to manage is somewhere between fifty and a hundred. When I combine both my personal and professional accounts, I have closer to three hundred different places that require me to enter a user name and password. How many do you have? Even on the low end, twenty-five to fifty unique user names and passwords are way too many for a human being to manage securely.

As I mentioned earlier, passwords are just one factor of authentication. So, what does one single factor actually get you? It only proves that the person or machine entering the code knows the secret. It does not prove that the person or machine is authorized to know that secret. While some security experts believe that frequently changing passwords and having complex passwords ensures authentication by making it much harder for hackers to discover their password, that really does very little. With the tools hackers have at their disposal, they can know a new password almost as soon as the user generates it.

The Missing Link

Another problem with today's password security is that the onus is on the user to maintain strong security practices. Think about it. Have you ever used the same password more than once? Written them down or typed them into a spreadsheet? Or used something like your child's birthday? How many times a day do you think employees and end-users circumvent security for their personal convenience? Virtually every computer user and company in the world face this serious problem. Unfortunately, nearly all of them have their heads in the sand about their most overlooked and under-solved problem. The missing link in network cybersecurity is an integrated set of tools that make passwords both secure and manageable *for the user*.

Humorous Ways Users Manage and Generate Passwords

After being in the password authentication business a very long time, I have collected a long list of zany ways people manage their passwords. One of the most common is the Word document or Excel spreadsheet titled "Passwords" and placed on the computer desktop. Of course, no hacker breaking into their computer would ever find this document, let alone open it, right?

Then there is what I like to call "Sticky Note Security." This is the writing of passwords on sticky notes and placing them on the computer monitor for easy access. Users trying to create some sense of security may hide their notes under the keyboard. Writing down passwords may free users from trying to remember all of their passwords, but then they have to remember where they hid them.

A few years back, the CEO of a marketing firm bet me a steak dinner that I could not find any of his employees' passwords because he had a written policy against writing them down. Not wanting to miss a dinner at Ruth's Chris, and hoping that he really did have security in place, I took the bet. To give him even better odds of winning, I let him choose which employee's cubical I was to search.

In less than two minutes, I found the password-laden sticky note hiding under the tissue box on the bookshelf. Over a juicy, medium rare, sixteen-ounce prime rib, we talked about how to improve his network security. The policy is not the challenge, it's the implementation.

I came across another example of poor password management in a slight variation of sticky note security. An executive at a large hotel chain wrote all her passwords on her white board. According to her, since hidden sticky notes will be found, and replacing them only adds to the landfill, she might as well make log-on easier on herself by just writing them on the white board in front of her desk.

The way employees generate passwords is equally creative. There's a joke going around that when I asked a client what his password was, he answered, "MickeyMinnieDonaldPlutoDocSleepyHappyDopey." When I asked why such a weird password, he replied, "It has to be eight characters long." While that may sound goofy, it's even worse when people use their anniversary date, kids' names, or the place where they met their spouse. All that information can usually be found by hackers in employees' Facebook, Google+, Twitter, or some other social media profile.

Here are some other similarly absurd password recommendations from so called "password experts:"

- Find a book title, poem, phrase, or favorite quote and then use the first letter of each word of the phrase or quote. According to the expert, you now have a complex password you can remember. What's wrong here is that the same password will be used at multiple sites; otherwise, the user has to remember a different quote for each site.

- Another one is to replace a known password with the letter in the alphabet just to the right or left of each character. I don't know about you, but when I sit down at a computer, the last thing I want to do is run a cipher algorithm in my head. Besides, even the entry-level hacker knows this trick and has automated tools that check for it.

- Perhaps the most ridiculous one is where the user picks the password based on the site's log-on message. When you visit a site, the screen might say, "Please enter password." So the password the user types in is, "PleaseEnterPassword." To keep passwords unique, they might choose,

"GooglePleaseEnterPassword" and "AmazonPleaseEnterPassword." While it meets most of the password requirements, it's another well-known trick.

These examples would be funnier if they weren't true. Generating and managing passwords is extremely important. These examples hopefully show you just how poorly your employees do it.

How Are Your Passwords Protected?

Many IT administrators will protect their password database the same way they protect all their other data. The data are stored behind a firewall, may require another password to access it, and are on the same server that also stores the company's marketing collateral, general reports, and other non-critical data. If the main goal is to prevent password theft, why would the password data file be stored on the same server that requires very limited security?

A more security-conscious IT manager will build on additional layers of security. They realize that at some point, a hacker may get the password data. The next layer of security should make the data unreadable and worthless. Here is where data encryption is applied. The savvy IT manager will implement encryption, hashing, and a host of other technologies that I will explain in a later chapter, and will also have a dedicated server just for passwords and other log-on credential information. Segregating sensitive data allows IT to monitor access, watch for anomalies like excessive pinging, and block URLs that are suspicious. By segregating data, IT can better monitor and prevent attacks, which could otherwise get lost in the noise of non-critical traffic.

⠿ SOMETHING TO THINK ABOUT

Recently a healthcare center IT administrator, who wishes to remain anonymous, did an independent network security audit. After a few hours of testing, the auditor presented his findings. The provider received a failing grade. However, they passed the government's HIPAA compliancy requirements because their security policies and procedures were all documented. The problem was that IT failed to monitor how their employees actually implemented and managed those policies. It was discovered that every healthcare worker used the exact same password: "Nurse123." The IT administrator could never truly authenticate a user, and if there ever was a breach, the audit reports would be useless.

The main disjoint between policies and implementation is the human factor. While it is true that long, complex, unique passwords that change frequently offer greater security, an employee frustrated with trying to remember all his passwords will do silly things that circumvent security for convenience. That is what hackers exploit.

These examples remind me of an old saying: "Computer security is easy. That is, easy to do poorly." Whatever issue you're dealing with, remember to ask yourself, "Are these password *authentication* problems? Or are they password *management* problems?

Laying the Foundation

Before jumping into how to create the Password Authentication Infrastructure (PAI) that meets your specific needs, I first want to build a foundation. All infrastructures bring together multiple components. Each component has its own strengths and weaknesses. The goal is to capitalize on one component's strength and then leverage in other components that address remaining weaknesses.

Cybersecurity infrastructure systems include the following elements:

- Ciphers
- Safeguarding Secrets
- Authorization
- Multi-factor Authentication
- Secure Hardware Modules
- Secure Channels of Communications

After a brief overview of each of these components, I will show you how easily you can incorporate these same principles into password security.

The best way to implement security is to first understand the attacks and methods hackers use against the different security components. In the next chapter, the flaws in current attempts at password security will become very clear, along with how PAI addresses each of them.

Finally, security implementation involves more than just technology. There is a business component that has to justify IT expenditures to the CFO and CEO.

That's why I also cover the return on investment (ROI) for password authentication security in a later chapter.

It is only when security is designed with a holistic, comprehensive approach that security really works. Nothing can be left to chance or taken for granted. And while no security system will ever be completely foolproof, when enough security layers are implemented, most hackers get frustrated by the barriers and go elsewhere. Layered security also gives IT more time to discover anomalies and kick out intruders before a breach occurs.

CHAPTER 3

THE WORLD OF CIPHERS

"There are two types of encryption: one that will prevent your sister from reading your diary and one that will prevent your government."

~ Bruce Schneier, American cryptographer

Frequently, I hear security experts comparing password security to other computer authentication solutions like Digital Certificates and Public Key Infrastructure (PKI). Many of these comparisons are misguided, and even wrong. My main dispute is that they are comparing a single factor of authentication (passwords) to an entire authentication infrastructure (like PKI) which is made up of a number of hardware, software, third-party verifications, and policies. They might as well compare a bicycle tire to a Ferrari.

Before I point out the errors in their logic, I first want to give some background and insight into how PKI infrastructures work, the components utilized, and the underlying security principles. Only a single component of a system should be compared with the singular component called passwords. After building a secure password authentication infrastructure with hardware, software and policies, then you can draw fair comparisons to other infrastructures.

In this section, I will describe one-way hash functions, symmetric encryptions like Data Encryption Standard (DES) and Advanced Encryption Standard (AES), and finish up with asymmetric encryption, which is found in Public/Private Key pairs. Rest assured, I will not go into long mathematical descriptions of how these algorithms work, but rather what makes these solutions popular and secure. You will also learn what their shortcomings are and what password management can learn from them.

Before I start, there is one other point that I would like to make very clear. To a computer, all data are just a series of zeros and ones. A password is like a secret key, which is like a Private Key, which is like a biometric template. They are all just a stream of zeros and ones. Below is a simple explanation of what makes each strategy unique.

Hash Function

The most common form of encryption involves the use of a hash algorithm. Hashing is a one-way encryption algorithm that takes any size block of data and generates a single unique value based on the placement of all the letters, spaces, and punctuations. In theory, the odds of any two blocks of data generating the same hash valuation are virtually nil. If a single period is out of place, the new hash valuation will be significantly different.

Another positive attribute of hashes is that they are a "one-way function." A text file can be turned into a single valuation, but the process cannot be reversed in order to cause the valuation to recreate the original text. Hashing is only used to determine message integrity. Hash valuations are never secret, and the algorithms are public knowledge. These facts may appear to make hashing sound insecure, but, as you are about to see, it's not.

The most commonly used hashes are Message-Digest (MD5), Secure Hash Algorithms (SHA-1 and SHA-2), and bcrypt. What determines the security of a hash is the insertion of a secret value called a "seed" or "key." Without knowing the seed, it is virtually impossible to generate the same valuation from the same message. When a person sends a message along with the hash value, and a receiver takes that message and re-runs the hash, the sender and receiver hash values must match. If one character is out of place, the hash value will not be the same. When hash values match, then you know the message was not changed during transmission. This gives you message integrity. This integrity is maintained by keeping the seed secret.

A security flaw with hash functions like SHA and MD is that the same hash seed, no matter when or by whom it was done, will generate the exact same hash value. For example, if the password "qwerty" generates a hypothetical value 135, and a million people are using the same "qwerty" password with the same seed within the same password database, there will be one million entries with the value 135. Given the same seed, whenever these words are hashed and no matter how often they are used, they will always generate the exact same valuation. A hacker only needs to try different seeds until he is able to recreate the 135 value from the word "qwerty." Once the hacker has the hash seed, he can start breaking other passwords. To solve this problem, cryptologists have come up with "Salting" the hash.

Salting the hash is a process in which every hash value is calculated using a unique seed. This can be done a couple of different ways. First, the seed can be a unique identifier found within a user's computer. While this may sound secure since access to the computer is required, today's hackers can easily discover this seed. Another downside about using a computer seed is that the user is tied to that one computer, since that is where the seed is located. Any other computer will deny access because the hash will not be the same, even though the password was typed correctly. This is very frustrating for mobile users. The only way to resolve this is to have multiple hash values for the same user for the same password.

The preferred way is to use a token or credential that is always in the individual's possession. I personally like the employee ID badge. Most employee badges contain some technology (typically a magnetic stripe, RF coil, and/or smartcard chip) that already has a unique identifier. When a credential is presented to any computer at the same time as a password, it is hashed the same way each time, but with a seed that is unique to and in possession of the individual. When hashes are salted, if a password data file is stolen and again, all million people on it used the password "qwerty," the file would have one million different hash value entries for the exact same password. And in case you were wondering, "qwerty" is a popular password because it's the first six letters on the top left of every keyboard.

It fascinates me that even today, with all the reports of passwords being compromised, some of the most frequently used passwords are still: "password," "12345," and "qwerty." In January of 2016, SplashData released their annual list of the Worst Passwords of 2015. While the three I just mentioned are all still in the top five, there were a few new entries to the most popular list: at #19, "letmein"; at #20, "login"; and #25, "starwars." This again demonstrates that user convenience trumps security.

Symmetric Ciphers and Keys

'Encryption' and 'cipher' are just fancy terms used to describe an advanced mathematical algorithm that is able to take readable text, scramble up its letters to make it unreadable, and then put it back to its original text by only those authorized to read it. Most people are familiar with symmetric ciphers because they are the process used in code books, Captain America decoder rings, and the WWII

Enigma machine. The way symmetric ciphers work is that all authorized users must share the same secret (or as we say in the cryptographic world, the same "secret key") to encrypt and decrypt.

The German electro-mechanical Enigma machine first introduced the world to the terms "settings," "rotors," and "keys." Rotor dials were set on the encoding machine to a specific key value that would then use very complex means to calculate a letter substitution code. There were 159 million million million possible settings, which were changed every day. In other words, there were more permutations than people on the planet.

What eventually broke Enigma were two things: technology and human errors (social engineering.) Brilliant work by the mathematicians John Jeffreys, Peter Twinn and Alan Turing at Bletchley Park unraveled the German administrative key. Alan Turing and Gordon Welchman created a computer nicknamed The Bombe that was able to cycle through all permutations in twenty minutes. The other breakthrough was the realization that almost every German transmission ended with "Heil Hitler." This human habit allowed the cryptologists to know they had the correct key when they got this phrase. I would argue that while The Bombe was necessary, it was ultimately human errors and habits that brought down Nazi security. Unfortunately, the same thing happens today with the way people manage their passwords.

With the advancement of computers, ciphers now use keys that are thirty-two characters long (256-bits) from a list of 256 unique characters wielding over 1.15×10^{77} combinations (that's 115 followed by seventy-five zeros!) While all this may sound secure and impressive, there is one Achilles' heel. Like Enigma, the protection of the shared secret Key is paramount. The possible unauthorized disclosure of this Key keeps cryptologists and engineers up at night.

Advantages - The advantages of symmetric ciphers are that they are relatively easy to implement, very fast to encrypt/decrypt, and they work very well on large amounts of data like paragraphs, chapters, or entire books. It would probably take a high-powered computer a day or two to encrypt the entire Library of Congress.

Disadvantages - The main disadvantage is managing all the secret keys. Everyone who needs to read a message must know the key. If you have multiple parties that you wish to communicate with, but only certain parties need to read the encrypted message, then you will need more keys. The more communication channels there are, the more keys you require. The more keys there are, the more complex the infrastructure. The more complex the infrastructure becomes, the more vulnerable points there are for hackers to attack. Finally, if keys need to change frequently, you now have the headache of transmitting new keys and the enormous hassle of managing who has what key, when they got it, and where they used it.

⬚ SOMETHING TO THINK ABOUT

If there are only two people (Alice and Bob) who need to communicate, then only one Key is required. Let's say they bring on a partner, Charlie. Now you have Alice who wants to send a message only to Bob, a different message only to Charlie, and a message that includes both Bob and Charlie. Alice just went from one Key to three. Finally, there is also the Bob-Charlie Key so Alice is kept out, for a total of four different Keys IT has to protect. Remember, symmetric Keys are shared, so an Alice-Bob Key is the same as a Bob-Alice Key.

Because this is a thriving business, they now hire Doug. Now we have eleven different keys (A-B, A-C, A-D, A-B-C, A-B-D, A-C-D, B-C, B-D, B-C-D, C-D, and A-B-C-D). A fifth employee makes the number now twenty-two separate Keys to manage. Now imagine if there are ten employees, a hundred employees, or three hundred million (as in the US population) and you begin to understand that it quickly becomes nearly impossible to manage and protect all those Keys.

But wait, we're not done. Imagine that all those Keys are changed every day. Now you get an understanding of the level and expense of technology required for Key management.

Secret Key Practices

Okay, brace yourself. I am about to get a little technical. I promise to keep the following descriptions as simple as possible. If you are looking to implement cybersecurity, it's good to have a general overview of what's out there so that no salesperson can pull the wool over your eyes. Hang in there. And, you're welcome.

Symmetric ciphers are algorithms that are dependent on a single shared Key called the "Secret Key" used for both encryption and decryption. This Secret

Key is not unlike a password. It is long, complex, unique, frequently changed, made up of a string of zeros and ones, and shared with at least one other person or machine.

The mathematical complexity of the Secret Key keeps it safe from brute-force attacks. However, there are other issues. The following details how Key security is accomplished.

Key Generation:

Computers generate Keys using complex mathematical equations to prevent unauthorized individuals from recreating or generating a fraudulent Key, and to make the Key very strong. The main point is that at no time does an end-user ever generate, know, or type any Secret Key, if for no other reason than it's just too long and complex. Technology does it for them. That adds to security because the best-kept secret is the one nobody knows.

Key Complexity:

Symmetric Keys have to be complex and long to make guessing or testing every possible combination nearly impossible. Complexity is based on both length and character types used. For example, a five-digit Key using only ten numeric characters (0-9) will generate a hundred thousand combinations. Compare that to a five-digit Key using a twenty-six character alphabet (A-Z) which will generate over eleven million combinations. The longer and more complex the Key, the less likely a brute force attack will work. Today, a typical symmetric Key is at least 256-bits or thirty-two characters long.

Key Exchange:

Symmetric encryption relies on keeping the Secret Key out of an enemy's hands by only letting the authorized person(s) know the Key. Throughout history, cryptographers have implemented a number of clever Key exchange schemes and devices, including a messenger who would rather die than reveal the secret (these people are hard to find today,) a code within a code, a Cryptex box, and steganography (hiding a message with a message).

Even today, with all our sophisticated computers, secure Key exchange is very important. Diffie-Hellman Key exchange, created in 1976, is a very effective way to exchange Secret Keys while keeping eavesdroppers from intercepting the

Key. Another common Key exchange is implementing asymmetric encryption for secure transmission of the Symmetric Key. Both these methods are used for secure Internet communication protocols. Both SSL (Secure Socket Layer) and HTTPS utilize these methods. You know they are in use when you see "HTTPS" associated with the URL in your Web browser's address bar.

Key Lifetime:

When it comes to cybersecurity, there are two approaches: Perfectly Secure or Practically Secure. The cost and effort to create Perfectly Secure is unrealistic. Practically Secure is good enough when the time it takes to break a Key is longer than the usefulness of the information. For example, the Duke of Wellington's battle plans would have been important to Napoleon on June 17, 1815. On June 18, 1815, the battle plans were useless.

A cryptologist knows that given enough time, money, and resources, an enemy could break a Secret Key. Periodic Key obsolescence neutralizes an enemy's Key-hacking efforts. The importance and usefulness of information determines a Key's life span. Some Keys are for one-time usage, while others can last for a few months or even years.

Unique Keys:

Symmetric encryption requires the creation of unique Secret Keys for use with each different person or group, as described earlier. As the number of connections increases, the addition of Keys grows exponentially. When the number of Keys becomes astronomical, the required node management and massive computer storage make networks extremely complex and expensive. However, with computers and advanced electronics managing all these Keys, the quantity of Keys has very few limitations. The take-away here is that machines, not humans, are better at managing Keys.

Key Storage:

At some point, all those Secret Keys have to be stored somewhere. Whether you are relying on the memory of a person, a code written on self-destruct paper, or a password in a computer database, security is only as strong as its weakest link. If Secret Keys are not securely stored, all the work generating sophisticated ciphers and unique, complex Keys with a short lifecycle is useless. A computer's weakest link is its data storage.

Today, the industry stores Secret Keys in smartcards, secure access modules (SAM), and hardware security modules (HSM.) These hardware devices use many advanced detectors, filters, and features to prevent most known attacks. Unfortunately, potential vulnerabilities will continue to exist as long as hackers are out there creating new threats.

Challenge-Response for Mutual Authentication:

After generating, distributing, and storing all the Symmetric Keys, how do you know that two computers are the correct ones to be communicating with each other? Challenge-Response establishes trusted communication through mutual authentication. Most networks utilize Challenge-Response technology to authenticate each other by testing if they know the same secret and have the same algorithm to correctly encrypt and decrypt data before sending.

Generally, Device 1 will first send a unique identifier to Device 2. Then Device 2 combines its own identifier with that from Device 1, runs the number through an algorithm, and calculates a unique value. Next, repeat the same process but in the opposite direction with a unique identifier flowing from Device 2 to Device 1. If both calculate the same value, then a trusted communication channel is established. Challenge-Response is a Key component in secure SSL and HTTPS network communication.

Kerberos is the most common Internet Challenge-Response protocol, but it is not the only one. The unique identifier (or "seed") can be a password, hash, random number, Secret Key, or some other unique value. The main requirement is that the two devices calculate the same value. Once the trusted connection is established, log-on and data transmission to Websites, applications, and networks can proceed. With spam emails and phishing and pharming attacks running rampant, all computers *must* establish secure mutual authentication.

Lessons Password Authentication Can Take From Symmetric Keys

Passwords and Symmetric Secret Keys are virtually identical in that they rely on the sharing of a secret. In order to keep symmetric ciphers secure, engineers have utilized many security techniques—all of which passwords can also utilize. The main difference between these two secrets is that employees do not generate or manage Keys. So, why should they generate and manage passwords?

By transferring many of the same security practices found in Secret Key operations to password management, you begin building the foundation of a Password Authentication Infrastructure (PAI).

Here is how you can adopt the elements that make Secret Keys secure and utilize them to make passwords secure:

Generation:

Because passwords do not use ciphers, they do not need complex generating algorithms. A password generator simply needs to allow for length, character types, complexity, and frequent change. Most computers have random number generator functions. Using these requires no additional software or programs.

Complexity:

A strong password also depends on complexity and length. Utilizing all ninety-six keyboard characters, an eight-character password would create over six quadrillion (six followed by fifteen zeros) combinations. That's impossible for a human to break by brute force, but not for a computer. To match the security of a Secret Key, a 32-character password is required. A 32-character password using just the standard ASCII characters (128 of them) creates about 2.7×10^{67} (27 followed by sixty-six zeros) combinations, which would take a computer doing one million tries per second about 8.5×10^{53} years to generate all possible combinations using a brute force attack! When the user does not need to remember or type their password, then length and complexity are no longer an issue.

Exchange:

Passwords themselves typically do not flow unencrypted across a network. Instead, computer networks transmit the password's hash and compare it to the hash stored on a site's server. Hashing by itself is no longer secure because every occurrence of a particular password, no matter the user, will have the same hash value. To keep the data flow secure, more and more Websites are implementing secure HTTPS protocols. However, companies still need to "salt" each hash separately. Then, identical passwords will have completely different hash values.

Passwords can also utilize Diffie-Hellman, asymmetric encryption, or SSL to securely exchange password data. As with Symmetric Key exchange, the goal is to hide the secret from unauthorized people.

Lifetime:

Passwords must have a defined end of life. Most security experts put an eight-character password at thirty to ninety days. A 32-character password can go much longer, assuming other password security mechanisms are in place. Alternatively, if the computer generates and manages passwords, taking employees completely out of the security equation, it becomes very easy to implement a 32-character-long password that can be changed every week, day, hour, or even minute. These lifetimes would seriously complicate life for hackers.

Computers make Symmetric Key lifecycles manageable by automatically generating the new Key. So why not have computers generate random passwords? Taking the burden of password generation and lifetime away from the user adds to the security of passwords, making them just as viable as Symmetric Keys.

Uniqueness:

IT managers will tell you that every Website, server, application, and computer needs its own unique password. If technology makes Symmetric Key nodes manageable, why not use similar technologies (like smartcards) to manage passwords? By removing the burden of password management, users will have to manage only their accounts, leaving security in the hands of IT where it belongs.

Storage:

Secret Keys are not some super-advanced piece of information that is inherently secure. They are the result of a combination of management and supporting technologies, which together maintain security and trust. Passwords are no different. Implementing smartcards and secure hardware modules to protect passwords raises them to a higher level of security.

Secret Key security is not achieved by picking and choosing only a few of these methods. Security relies on implementing all the components together, leveraging each component's strength, while negating any weaknesses with one of the other components. This leveraging creates an infrastructure. To create a secure Password Authentication Infrastructure (PAI), all the same components used to create and manage Secret Keys must be utilized.

Asymmetric Ciphers and Keys

Asymmetric ciphers are unique because instead of one Key, there are two: a Public Key and a Private Key. These two Keys are mathematically tied together so you can use one Key to encrypt and only its sister Key to decrypt. Different security needs dictate which Key is appropriate for encrypting and which for decrypting. Asymmetric ciphers create options that no other cipher can.

The Public Key is like a name in a phone book. Everyone can see it and access the information. The Private Key, on the other hand, must be kept secret and very secure. For the security of the encryption to be maintained, it must never be revealed or compromised. Engineers exercise great effort and expense to maintain Private Key security utilizing smartcards, hardware security modules, special blade servers, and much more.

Asymmetric ciphers allow the user to safeguard either who is allowed to read a message or who sent the message. The user accomplishes this by choosing which Key (Public or Private) they use to encrypt.

The three trust models are:

1. **Trusted Receiver:** If I encrypt a message with your Public Key, only your Private Key will decrypt it. Since only you have possession of your Private Key, I know you are the only one who can read my message.

2. **Trusted Sender:** If I encrypt with my Private Key, which only I possess, then the message I send out can be read by anyone who uses my Public Key. This proves only I could have sent it.

3. **Trusted Storage:** Finally, if I encrypt with my Public Key, I can now safeguard my stored data because only my Private Key will decrypt it.

The security concerns regarding any Private Key are:

- Brute-force attack

- Discovery of the Private Key from the Public Key

- Duplication of a Private Key from a similar Public Key

- Theft

This is why so many different technologies and products are specifically combined to secure that Private Key. These safeguards are no different from the ones used to protect Symmetric Secret Keys. So, why not use them to protect passwords? Secure authentication, no matter the means, is only as secure as the protection of its secrets.

Advantage - The advantage of an asymmetric cipher is Key management and message trust. Users only need one Key to access everything, and trust is determined by which Key is used. This universal, single-Key idea is what makes people gravitate to these ciphers as a replacement to passwords. However, when theory meets practice, a different realization often occurs.

Disadvantages - The disadvantages of asymmetric ciphers are that they are very mathematically intensive and require a lot of computer computational power. Because advanced mathematics are utilized, additional cryptographic co-processors are required, which drives up implementation costs. Finally, asymmetric ciphers are very slow at encrypting and decrypting data. For that reason, they are typically only used for small bytes of data like a word or two instead of blocks, as described with symmetric ciphers.

In Chapter 8, I discuss infrastructures that take advantage of both symmetric and asymmetric ciphers to eliminate the weaknesses of both ciphers while capitalizing on each of their strengths.

Asymmetric Key generations use one of two mathematical principals: RSA, which requires logarithms and prime numbers, or Elliptic Curve Cryptolography (ECC), which uses algebra and binary shifting. Unless you are heavy into mathematics, you don't need to understand the difference, just that the result is Key generation. RSA takes much longer and requires special (more costly) processors than does ECC.

Following is how Public/Private Key pairs are managed:

Key Generation:

The complex mathematics that goes into generating a Key pair is beyond the scope of this book. What is important is understanding the amount of computation overhead required to generate some Keys. For example, RSA cryptography uses prime numbers, logarithms, and exponentials. As the number sequence increases, the difficulty of finding new prime numbers also increases. While there might not be a finite number of prime values, the size of a prime number may be too large for effective use. The second issue with RSA is the intense mathematical processing required for logarithmic and anti-logarithmic calculations. This is often compounded when many requests come in at the same time, which overload a normal server. To solve this problem, advanced mathematic co-processors or specialized mathematical blade servers are required. All this comes at a substantial additional financial investment that many companies simply cannot afford.

The premise of Elliptic Curve Cryptography (ECC), given a random closed curve (ellipse) with an infinite number of points and a known point on that curve, is that it's very difficult to find its correct reflection point used to generate the Key. Granted, I am oversimplifying the explanation here, but the beauty of ECC is that it requires no prime numbers and uses basic algebraic calculations that any simple computer processor can do. ECC generates Keys faster and stronger, and with less computational overhead than RSA. Reportedly, a 256-bit ECC Key is comparable to a 3072-bit RSA Key in strength and magnitude, as well as being faster to calculate.

No matter which cipher is used, there are mathematical equations and algorithms required to generate Key pairs that are tied together. While there is no theoretical reason why one could not frequently change the Key pair, it becomes more of a practical problem. When Keys are changed, it requires processing time, the Key management of knowing which Key pair was used on which document, and the storage of older pairs for the recovery of older messages.

Key Complexity:

One of the major concerns in determining Key length is the time it takes to discover a Private Key by means of a brute-force attack. The limited number of available prime numbers, high computational speeds of computers, and an increasing number of certificate requests also contribute to the ever-increasing Key length. That's why the accepted length of an RSA-generated Private Key today is now 2048-bits (or 256 characters.) In the not so far-off future, the acceptable length will grow to 4096-bits. Key length also affects the time it takes to generate a digital signature, requiring more memory storage space on the smartcard, which translates into higher costs for the smartcard.

Key Exchange:

Key exchange is relatively easy with PKI, which makes it attractive to CIOs and CISOs. The Private Key, which never gets distributed, is more secure when generated within the same device where it is going to be stored (e.g., within a smartcard or HSM.) However, if the Key is to be generated on one device and stored on another, then Key exchange solutions like Diffie-Hellman need to be invoked.

Key Lifetime:

Due to a Private Key's length and complexity (which makes them nearly impervious to brute-force attack), these Keys typically have a one- to five-year lifespan. However, the value of the information they protect will determine their lifespan.

As discussed earlier, because information that has been encrypted with one Key pair cannot be decrypted using a different pair, older Key pairs have to be kept accessible. I have frequently seen smartcard implementations where a card with 16K bytes of memory had been deployed because there was only one Key pair involved. But when it came time to change Keys, the smartcard did not have enough storage capacity. In addition to the cost of a new Key, a new smartcard with 32K of memory needed to be added. These cards cost more, and, IT then had two cards to manage, where there used to be one. Additionally, there is the whole issue of collecting old cards and reissuing new ones. Guess what happens when a third Key is required?

Unique Keys:

With both RSA and ECC, the two Keys are generated in such a way that both are long, complex, and unique. The potential number of possible pair combinations makes duplicate Key pairs virtually impossible.

Key Storage:

The safest Private Keys are those that are generated and stored in secure hardware like Hardware Security Modules (HSM) or smartcards. In these cases, the Private Key never leaves the device. Another way to look at this is that the user never even has the opportunity of knowing their Private Key.

If the Private Key inside an HSM cannot be exported or hacked, then the only way to steal the Key is to physically steal the HSM unit. This type of attack is less likely to go unnoticed. Plus, some HSM units have an auto-destruct mechanism. If power is removed or the unit is tampered with, the entire unit's memory is wiped out.

Smartcards can be lost or stolen more easily than an HSM. That is why most require additional authentications, like a PIN or biometric, before access is granted. Additional security in some smartcards includes a fuse inside the chip which is blown after too many incorrect PIN entries, permanently disabling the card. Smartcards also include other security features that can make probing for data far more expensive and time-consuming than the value of the information they protect. Hackers prefer to take the easiest and least expensive path.

Challenge-Response (C-R):

While it may be argued that when a user enters a password (challenge) and the computer checks it (response), that constitutes a C-R. However, there is a lot more to it.

In simple terms, mutual authentication between two devices happens when they exchange information that is then processed with secret information stored inside each of these devices. As previously described, each device calculates a unique value from this information. If both devices derive the same valuation, then it is assumed they both know the shared secret and are authorized to connect. One device can be a smartcard and the other a computer server.

Lessons Password Authentication Can Take from Asymmetric Keys

All the components used to safeguard Private Keys can also be used to protect passwords. Here are a few things that can and should be done:

Generation:

Remember my comment that a password, Secret Key, biometric template, and Private Key all look the same to a computer because they're just a long series of zeros and ones? The main feature that differentiates Keys, templates, and passwords is how they are generated. Passwords are the only one that humans are allowed to generate.

A password is the easiest and least expensive "Key" to generate because it requires no mathematical algorithms, no seed, no pairing to another password, and no secret information. All that is required for a long, complex, and very secure password is a simple random character generator.

There is an old security adage: "Security by Obscurity." This simply means if the attacker does not know how information was generated, then it cannot be replicated. Because passwords are not mathematically tied to anything like seeds or biometrics, they are completely obscure. Passwords can also be changed frequently without affecting anything else because they are used for authentication only and are <u>not</u> part of encryption ciphers that also require decryption.

Complexity:

Passwords do not need to be as large as an RSA Key. A 256-character password using all 128 ASCII characters would generate over 2.7×10^{539} (27 with five hundred and thirty-eight zeros behind it) combinations. In other words, it's a really, really big (virtually unhackable) number. To add a reference for that, there are only approximately 3×10^{11} stars in the Milky Way. With such a large number of possibilities and no need to rely on prime numbers or advanced math co-processors, a password can be much smaller than a Private Key and still take an unreasonable number of years to crack using a brute-force attack. The smaller password also allows for a much less expensive smartcard, because there is less storage capacity required.

Hackers don't just have super-fast computers, they also gang together a number of computers (called bots) to share the processing load. With this in mind, a strong password needs to be at least twelve characters long to make a brute-force attack unreasonable. Taking it a step further, the NIST (National Institute of Standards and Technology) Draft Special Publication 800-118 (April 2009) recommends that every password now needs to be at least 15 characters long. It amazes me that even the official Microsoft Website still offers "Tips for creating a strong password" that are rudimentary.

Exchange:

Contrary to popular belief, when you log into an account and type in your password, your actual password is not sent. Instead, the password you type is first hashed and then that hash is sent across the Internet. The receiving server then compares that hash value against the one stored in its database. If they match, you are in. Sending a hash led computer engineers to coin the term "Pass the Hash" (PtH).

Lifetime:

This has been an ongoing trade-off between security and user convenience. Changing passwords frequently makes them more secure, but trying to get users to remember the latest one is arduous. Just ask anyone working the IT help desk how many password resets they deal with daily. In a lame attempt to make passwords both secure and less cumbersome, the industry standardized the policy of eight characters with a life span of 30-90 days. Because Private Keys are much longer and secured by other technologies, they can have a longer lifecycle. It is my position that if passwords were longer and properly secured, they too could have a much longer lifecycle than the out of date, insecure, eight-character, user-generated password.

Uniqueness:

Unique passwords are easy to accomplish. They require no mathematical algorithms, and since there is no pairing, changing passwords is also easy and fast. Machine-generated passwords utilize the entire American Standard Code for Information Interchange (ASCII) set of 128 standard characters, or 256 if the extended characters are included. In comparison, a standard keyboard has only ninety-two symbols a user can easily type. Therefore, a machine-generated password will be far more complex and unique than what a person could type and remember.

Storage:

A secure password manager uses technologies similar to those used by asymmetric Keys to generate and store passwords. By taking the human element out of the security chain, IT is able to remove its biggest vulnerability. When passwords are stored in similar devices, they are just as secure as a Private Key. Security is not defined by the methodology but by the secure management of the methodology. When passwords are just as difficult to crack or discover as a Private Key, then they are just as secure.

Challenge-Response (C-R):

Today's computer security experts are pushing for network mutual authentication *before* the firewall and before access to any data. When C-R enabled smartcards are used, they ensure that the chip and server verify each other. The server verifies the chip and the chip verifies the server. Challenge-Response will protect password entry, password data files, and guard against many computer attacks.

Now that you know the basic ciphers and their components, let's talk about the importance of Authentication.

CHAPTER 4

AUTHENTICATION

"Social Security Number Cards by themselves were never intended to be personal identity documents because they cannot confirm that a person presenting a card is actually the person whose name appears on the card."

~ Ron Lewis, former member,
United States House of Representative

Authentication is the process of establishing that a person or computer really is who they claim to be. When authentication is ignored or poorly implemented, you leave the virtual front door unlocked for hackers and other unauthorized entities.

In the physical world where someone deals with the same people day in and day out, a guard will start to recognize faces, voices, and mannerisms. Soon, a person can get past the gatekeeper with a wave and a "good morning." But when a stranger approaches, the gatekeeper becomes more alert and asks to see some identification. After several visits, the gatekeeper establishes familiarity and will often revert to simple facial recognition.

In the digital world, human-to-human recognition is not possible. The digital world can only operate remotely with people and machines both across the hall and halfway around the world. The challenge for a computer network is to accurately authenticate an individual before they are allowed past the virtual front door, also known as your firewall. To resolve this dilemma, the security industry has established three means (called "factors") to authenticate the true identity of someone or something. The three factors are Knowledge, Possession, and Inherence.

Knowledge Factor (Something you Know)

The something a person or device can know include a Personal Identification Number (PIN), password, Key, or challenge phrase. A visitor presents this information, usually by typing, submitting, or speaking the information they know.

A machine can possess knowledge just as easily as a person can. No matter who or what submits pass code information, there must be trust that the information being supplied is not only correct, but also submitted by the real authorized person or entity. When that trust is absent, only a limited number of incorrect attempts should be allowed before barriers slam shut.

> **Advantages** - Knowledge-based factors are the most common and least expensive to implement, and over 90% of all computers, networks and applications use this type of authentication. Usually, only software has to be added or activated for deployment.
>
> Another advantage is that known elements are easy to change. A simple request allows either a computer to generate a new password or a user to click a button and change their password. Resetting passwords takes just seconds, typically at no expense.
>
> Finally, known elements can be changed frequently. This is the most important advantage of known elements over all other authentication factors. Changing a password can happen manually or automatically every year, week, day or second. As you will see in the other factors described below, change can be difficult, expensive, or even impossible.
>
> **Disadvantage** - The biggest weakness with knowledge-based factors is the human element. Most humans can only remember so many different passwords, and only so many different characters. When people are put in charge of this factor, it automatically becomes the weakest link in your chain of trust. If a password is easy for a person to remember and type, it's safe to assume that it will be easy for a hacker to discover.

Another weakness with knowledge systems is that the knowledge has to be stored. If the storage security is weak, then a hacker can steal it. This is an important consideration because knowledge only proves that someone or something knows the secret. It does not prove that they are authorized to know it. When a correct user name and password are entered, no matter who enters them, the network cannot see this as a breach. As long as they have the correct password, IT cannot stop an unauthorized visitor from getting past their firewall.

Possession Factor (Something you Have)

This factor is all about having a physical item that only authorized people or computers possess. It might be a key, tamper-proof picture ID, magnetic stripe card, smartcard (contact and contactless), USB token dongle, key fob, mobile phone, and the list goes on. Security is achieved by making these items special and unique to avoid cloning or copying, and they are issued only by approved organizations, which establishes the authentication trust.

Smartcards (credit card size, plastic credentials) are used in a majority of installations. A card can have the photo and name of an employee printed on it, while special anti-cloning graphics, RFID, magnetic stripe, and contact chips can all be combined on one card for multi-application functionality. They are lightweight and relatively inexpensive.

> **Advantages** - A company's physical security or HR department issues ID badges only to people they know they have hired. These tokens are also serialized, so security knows how many have been issued, lost, stolen, and replaced. Finally, because there is a limited number of tokens issued, security is achieved through scarcity.

> When the token is a card, then additional personalization features can be added (photos, logos, holograms, and names). Even something as common as a credit card has security features incorporated during its manufacture to make it difficult to copy.

> Issuance is also easy. Cards are either handed out, or they may be mailed.

> Depending on the security features and technologies within the credential, they are fairly inexpensive to manufacture and purchase.

And, there are a number of manufacturers around the world that can make them.

Over the years, the card industry has developed many high-security features that make cloning cards virtually impossible. We have all seen the special hologram images embedded in credit cards. But, did you know about ultraviolet inks, micro printing, guilloche patterns, hidden images, and color-shifting inks? While these features will add to the cost of the card, each issuer has to determine specific priorities relative to card cost versus a security breach.

Disadvantages - Physical items can be lost, stolen, or forgotten. This becomes a management issue. Unlike the knowledge factors, which can easily be changed, possession requires logistics of purchase, issuance, collection, re-issuance, and disposal management. This is why physical devices are infrequently changed.

Physical credentials have to be purchased and stocked. A card may cost $5, whereas a new smartphone can be $400. This determination will also dictate which device is appropriate for the given environment. Besides the cost and lead time to purchase more inventory, there is also the secure storage and issuance cost of that inventory. A smartcard deployment will also require software and readers.

Once again, the human factor raises the question of how well a user or employee safeguards their credential. If the replacement process is easy and painless for the user, and they have no personal skin in the game to protect the token, they are sometimes left lying around for hackers or thieves to steal. Anything physical can be stolen.

All a credential does is prove that the person has that credential in their possession. If it is not personalized, there is no way to know if an individual is authorized to have that credential.

⊞ SOMETHING TO THINK ABOUT

Almost every employee carries an ID badge that also includes physical access. You know those door readers that beep when the badge is presented, unlocking the door? What is that process really proving? It proves nothing more than that the person is in possession of a working card. It does not prove they are the authorized holder of the card. That is why pictures and names are printed on cards. While a name and picture would not stop entry through an unmanned door, once inside, employees and security have the ability to compare the photo to the face.

Inherence Factor or Biometrics (Something you Are)

Biometrics has become very popular recently. Biometrics is the ability to use anatomical, physiological, or behavioral characteristics as unique identifiers of an individual. Some common examples include fingerprints, facial structure, hand geometry, iris, voice, and even vein recognition. Some of the more obscure methods include typing on a keyboard, handwriting, walking, and blood type. Probably not too far in the future (as soon as it becomes fast enough), DNA will be added to that list.

Since no two people in the world are born with these same feature patterns, theoretically, no two people are the same. Fingerprints are still the most commonly used biometric. Over the years, the cost of these readers has come down. Hand geometry readers are typically deployed for room access that has little traffic, but because these readers are big and bulky, they are not practical for computer access. With smartphones and tablets, including a built-in microphone and camera, voice and facial recognition has an advantage. Iris scanning is still one of the most expensive biometric readers.

The way biometrics works is that a reader scans features, like the types of swirls, islands, ridges, and valleys, and any other characteristic of a fingerprint. Then a computer running a proprietary algorithm takes all that data and generates a template (a mathematical valuation of the fingerprint, not the actual image). This template is just a long string of zeros and ones.

An analogy for this template might be to take a piece of tracing paper and lay it on top of the map of the United States. Then, for every city that begins with the letter "C," has an "o" in it, and has a population over 5,000 between the ages of 18 and 45, place a pinhole or dot there. Now remove the tracing paper, hand it to a complete stranger and ask him to use it to draw to scale the exact image of the original map that created the dots on the tracing paper.

Because a template is just a string of zeros and ones which have to be stored in a computer database, all a hacker has to do is steal the database and play back the template without the reader. While encryption may give the template some protection, the concern is, how is that done and how is it safeguarded? Encryption depends on the security of the Key it uses. How that Key is protected determines the security of the encrypted template. That Key can be a Secret Key, a Private Key, or even a password. A biometric template is non-reversible and cannot recreate the thing it came from, in this case, a fingerprint. So, is an encrypted fingerprint template really so different from a hashed password?

Hackers have been known to fool biometric readers. Lifting a fingerprint and transferring it to a gummy bear, and breathing on a sensor are just two of a number of clever means. One way the industry has tried to combat these attacks is to verify that the biometric is being presented by a live person. This might be temperature, elasticity of the skin, or even detecting a pulse. While these methods help, they raise the cost of the readers higher and higher.

The correct reading of a biometric is determined by the sensitivity threshold settings of the reader. Low settings will verify very quickly because they limit the number of matching points. High settings, on the other hand, can take longer to match, but give more accurate positive authentications. The verification setting depends on the security requirements of the environment.

After the desired setting is determined, there is a statistical probability of a wrong match or rejection called the False Acceptance/False Rejection (FAFR) ratio. This determines how many times an unauthorized person is wrongly authorized and admitted, versus an authorized person being denied access because the system did not recognize him. Lowering the sensitivity threshold will lower the number of false rejections but will also raise the number of false acceptances.

Time for authentication is also determined by the size of the database and where the comparison is being done. After a reader scans a fingerprint and generates a template, it now has to compare this value against every other entry. This process is called a one-to-many search. The number of entries and the complexity of the template will determine the authentication time. If a database contains hundreds of templates (or as in law enforcement, millions of templates,) it could take awhile. The way around this is to point the newly read fingerprint template to a specific person called a one-to-one search. In this case, you need an additional means to correctly point to the correct file.

The health of the individual and the environment will also affect the usefulness of biometrics. If someone has an injury to a finger, hand, or face, the template won't match. If the background noise is high, voice templates won't match. If it is cold outside and people are wearing gloves, templates won't match.

Other concerns that will also need to be addressed when deploying biometrics are proprietary solutions, limited cross platform access, enrollment procedures, sanitation of the reader, and more.

⊞ SOMETHING TO THINK ABOUT

The recent data breach at the U.S. Office of Personnel Management exposed the private and personal information of eighteen million current, former, and prospective federal employees, including those with top-secret clearances, government/military access, and a number of other rights and privileges that require the highest level of authentication. On the biometrics side, the thieves got actual images of fingerprints. With technology advances, it is not farfetched to believe that artificial fingers with legitimate fingerprints etched into them could be made to fool biometric authentication systems.

While biometric supporters like to argue that their sensors can distinguish between a live finger and a dead one, that protection is designed to prevent someone from chopping off fingers. But just how hard is it to fool these sensors? One example is the infamous gummy bear attack.

Tsutomu Matsumoto used gelatin (found in Gummi Bears®) to create a fake finger. Next, using cyanoacrylate (super-glue adhesive) fumes to enhance latent fingerprints on a glass, he lifted and photographed the fingerprint. Using Photoshop and a photosensitive printed-circuit board, Matsumoto created an etched fingerprint, and pressed it onto the gelatin finger to create a 3D representation of the print. This finger fooled fingerprint detectors about 80 per cent of the time.

The security argument comes down to the capabilities and sophistication of a biometric reader's sensors. With advanced synthetic materials now readily available, as well as etching techniques, simple software programs, and advances in 3D printing, it is not too hard to imagine a sophisticated prosthesis cloned to fool a sensor. If the Chinese (who are cited as the ones who hacked into the OPM) can break into our nation's computer, making a fake finger to fool commercial-grade sensors will be extremely easy.

Advantages - Everyone has unique biometric characteristics, so no two people are exactly alike. Your biometrics are always with you, and hopefully we don't get to the point where people start losing appendages so hackers can get someone's biometrics. Biometric characteristics are not something you can change either legally or without a lot of pain and money.

Disadvantages - Because biometrics cannot be changed easily, the next best attack point becomes changing the algorithm that generates the templates. With the sophistication of hackers today, how difficult do you think it would be to break into a computer network, alter the biometric template algorithm, and/or change the acceptance levels to make the computer think someone else is you? Or better yet, insert a new template file to include an unauthorized outsider?

If a company wanted to try to improve security by changing templates like they change passwords, they would do that by modifying the template seed value. Because biometric systems claim they do not store images, the only way to re-identify individuals is to re-enroll them. That is a cumbersome, if not almost impossible task for a very large organization.

Experts also like to claim that your biometrics are *always* in your possession. I take exception to that. For example, we leave our fingerprints behind almost everywhere we go. And as the gummy bear attacker showed, others can be in possession of the personal inherence factor known as your fingerprint.

Overall, biometrics has much to offer the security industry and should be considered where appropriate. However, the theft at the OPM shows me that biometrics, by itself, is not a foolproof method of authentication, and certainly not a replacement for the password.

Location Factor (Where you Are)

A fourth factor of authentication is emerging—Where you Are. With GPS, cellular, WiFi, and smart devices, it is now possible to use your location history for authentication. Imagine living in a small town where all your wireless devices communicate with a few regional cell towers. Suddenly, having an authentication request appear from North Korea... The odds are very high that it is fraudulent. Using location as a means of authentication has many social and privacy issues that are beyond the scope of this book. However, it is becoming more popular among security pundits.

Advantages - The Location Factor is similar in many aspects to biometrics in that it relates to your personal habits and privacy. Credit card companies have been using your buying and location habits for years to spot stolen card numbers and fraudulent purchases.

Disadvantages - If the battery in your phone dies, this authentication would no longer be available. Additionally, all this shows is the location of the device, not whose hand it is in. Therefore, using a location factor by itself is insecure.

Because this is still new, not all the disadvantages have been discovered. However, it makes you wonder who else is tracking your movements and how might they use this information.

All these factors of authentication are viable; however, each one by itself is weak and can be used fraudulently. That is why security experts agree that to truly authenticate an individual, you need to require at least two factors be present at the same time. This is referred to as multi-factor authentication (MFA).

CHAPTER 5

MULTI-FACTOR AUTHENTICATION (MFA)

*"Today we are using passwords, and they won't cut it.
We need to move to multifunction authentication. A
lot of that will be using a smart-card approach that
needs to be built down into the system."*

~ Bill Gates, Microsoft

Using only one of the four factors mentioned above is called Single-Factor Authentication (SFA). One factor alone is considered very weak authentication. Cards can be cloned, passwords cracked, biometrics fooled, and smartphones stolen. Multi-Factor Authentication (MFA) happens when the combination of two or more of these dissimilar methods are presented at the same time. What makes Multi-Factor Authentication secure is that the odds of a hacker being able to possess all the authentication components at the same time is extremely unlikely. To accomplish this would require more time, money, and sophistication than most hackers are capable of having. Plus, if the hackers are located in a foreign country, then it becomes virtually impossible, unless there are inside accomplices.

The combination of two or more of the <u>same</u> factor (like two cards, two passwords, or two biometrics) is not really multi-factor authentication. While this is stronger than only having one single factor, combining two of the same factor is referred to as "multi-single-factor authentication."

No one combination of factors is necessarily better than another. You have to determine which solution(s) work best in your specific environment(s).

Here are four tips you should consider when choosing which factors to combine:

- **User convenience:** This is placed first because no matter what any security technology promises, if the solution is cumbersome, users will find ways to circumvent it to make their life easier.

- **The value of the data:** Not all data is equally valuable. You would not pay $1,000 to secure something that's worth $5. Similarly, you should not pay $5 to secure something worth $1,000.

- **Support, Maintenance, and Training:** How much work is required by your IT staff to install, manage, and train for the system? IT convenience is also important.

- **Risk/Threat assessment:** You need to understand who might want your data and their level of sophistication.

I just want to repeat that there is no 100% secure solution. All that any cybersecurity system can do is put up enough barriers and monitors to prevent 98% of attacks. For most companies, that's good enough.

Two Factor Authentication (2FA)

Two Factor Authentication is the combination of any two of the factors. Because "Where you Are" is not yet fully accepted as a factor by the security community, I will not use it as an example.

Something you Have and Know:

This is the most common of all the two-factor systems. It is relatively inexpensive to deploy and manage. It uses much of a company's existing infrastructure, and is the least cumbersome for employees. The typical solution is an employee's badge and a password. The employee presents his card via a reader connected to the computer <u>and</u> types in a Personal Identification Number (PIN).

The system will read the unique identifier of the card and the PIN. Stronger systems will encode this information in ways that makes it very difficult to fool. The data will also be encrypted using SSL protocols before any data are transmitted to prevent data capture and playbacks.

Advantages - The cards can be magnetic stripe, contactless card, or even a contact smartcard that is also used for employee identification, physical access control, time and attendance record keeping, payment, and/or a number of other applications available that the company deems necessary.

The PIN can be fairly short to make it less burdensome for the user to type and remember.

Smartcards actually allow the match to occur within the card, so the user's known information is never stored in some offsite data center or server.

Disadvantages - The biggest threat to this particular 2FA is the disgruntled employee or insider. They can watch an employee type his or her PIN and later, steal the card.

Magnetic stripe ATM, credit, and debit cards face frequent and common attacks. Thieves place a second card reader called a skimmer inside the point of sale terminal and a small camera pointed at the keypad. When a card is swiped, the skimmer copies data from the card while the camera records the PIN entry. Then, the thief clones the magnetic stripe onto a blank card, which he can use or sell along with the PIN.

To prevent these attacks, the industry is moving to smartcards that are more difficult to clone. You have probably already received your new credit card with a shiny gold chip on it, though not all stores in the US are set up to use it yet.

⬛ SOMETHING TO THINK ABOUT

In October 2015, the United States officially switched from magnetic stripe credit cards to smartcards. The US is finally catching up to the Europeans with respect to EMV and "Chip 'n' PIN" security. Or, are they?

On October 3, 2015, I had a brief conversation with California Assemblymember Matt Dababneh of the 45th District about the new chip cards. He asked me if we (Congress) made a mistake by removing the PIN function. My answer was a resounding "Yes," and here's why.

1. The credit card industry still treats the smartcard as a single function, magnetic stripe replacement and not as a multi-function, multi-factor authentication token for the digital age.

2. Credit card companies and retail stores that issue their own cards want to protect their branding more than offering customer convenience. They do this by not allowing multiple accounts to all be stored on one card, especially not their card.

3. Now that you have your new chip cards, has the number of cards in your wallet decreased? Probably not. Recently I had to look into my wife's purse to find her car keys. (I like to tease her that I need someone to tie a rope around my waist before going in, just in case I get lost.) It was during my search that I found a four-inch plastic brick in her purse. It was all her loyalty and membership cards held together with a rubber band. One single smartcard could hold all of those and many more.

4. Card issuers often refuse to allow customers to change the chip's PIN to something they can remember. They use the argument that PINs would be set to easy numbers like phone numbers or birthdays that thieves could figure out. Probably true, but chips are way more sophisticated than the old magnetic stripe cards. They can be programmed to self-destruct if the wrong PIN is entered a pre-determined number of times. When issuers set your PINs for you, that leaves the user having to remember a different PIN for every card. Here comes the user password management nightmare all over again.

5. So instead of card issuers utilizing chip cards to increase security and tackle fraud (your high interest rates pay for their losses), they recommended to legislators that the PIN requirement in the US be dropped so customers would not have the burden of managing PINs. Our representatives went along with it.

6. Instead of getting a more secure "Chip 'n' PIN" technology, all we got was "Card 'n' Nothing."

7. All Congress did was kick the can down the road. Our new high tech credit cards have a vulnerability that the industry decided to ignore: authenticating the user to the credential. Your card is the Something you Have and your PIN is the Something you Know. Strangely, Congress turned off the security feature they mandated!

Allowing individuals to utilize the amazing capabilities of smartcards would put an end to issuer and store logos on cards. Imagine purchasing a blank card at any grocery store, custom printing it with your favorite images, and uploading the vast majority of account numbers on all those cards you currently carry in your wallet or purse. Having them all in one place, you could protect them all by memorizing one very secure PIN.

The smartcard is not a migration of magnetic stripe card technology. It's a migration of the computer. I believe if we are ever going to break away from single-function cards and go to multi-function cards, it will take the computer industry to do it. After twenty-five years in the smartcard industry, watching how poorly financial institutions have implemented smartcard technology, I really do believe their brand is more important to them than their customers' convenience or security.

Something you Have and Are:

This is similar to the Have and Know authentication, but instead of typing a PIN, you use your fingerprint, face, voice, or any other biometric. The user simply presents his card, then puts his finger on a scanner, looks into a camera, or speaks into a microphone.

With a smartcard, the biometric template can be stored on the card itself, not in some remote data center that hackers can target. Having a match-on-card solution ties the user to a specific card.

Advantages - Again, similar to the Have and Know advantages, but now the person doesn't need to remember anything. The person *is* the second factor.

Disadvantages - Biometrics exist as templates, so where the information is stored and how securely it is stored must be a consideration. Reader costs can be high, depending on quality. Low-quality readers may have higher False Acceptance/False Rejection (FAFR) ratios.

Something you Are and Know:

With this solution, a user presents his fingerprint, then types the PIN. Everything resides within the individual. There is no need to carry anything extra.

Advantages - With all the smartphones, tablets, kiosks, and other mobile devices we have today, the convenience of not having to plug in something more or worry that you forgot to bring your token is a big convenience advantage.

Extra devices can be lost, stolen, or forgotten. When employees come to work without their device, IT would have to offer the employee a recovery system allowing them to work when they are not in possession of their credential, or have a policy that they must return home and get their card or dongle. That is not a problem with this solution.

Disadvantages - Authentication information has to be stored in a central server somewhere. Whenever data is stored remotely, it is at risk of being stolen. If there is no central storage, then every terminal will require its own storage capability.

Three Factor Authentication (3FA)

As the name implies, this occurs when the Have, Know, and Are factors are all combined to produce the ultimate assurance of authentication. Again, the odds of a hacker having all three factors at once are significantly more remote than requiring just two. With this higher security comes greater cost, so before you implement 3FA, it is a good idea to first perform a risk and threat evaluation to ascertain the value of the data you are trying to protect.

Multiple Single-Factors Do <u>Not</u> Create Multi-Factor Authentication

I often come across products that claim to be multi-factor authentication which, in reality, are not. They simply use the same factor multiple times. For example, a system where you type in a password and then type in a code sent to your phone is actually "Double-Single-Factor Authentication." It's something you know (password), and something you know (code). Typing in multiple codes utilizes only one direct interface with one factor: the person. The smartphone is not entering the code, the person is. Some pundits argue that because the computer made the request to have the code sent to a specific phone that the computer did authentic it. I respectfully disagree.

Another example of Double-Single-Factor Authentication would be the use of both voice and facial recognition, which again are two Something you Are authentications. Some say it's just semantics, but I truly believe that understanding the finer points and properly implementing them is how you actually prevent a security breach.

Layers of Assurances

Layering multi-factor authentication also increases security. These layers of assurances look like this: The first layer consists of the user applying one set of multi-factor authentication, a card (Something the User Has) and a PIN (Something the User Knows,) which authenticate to the computer that the card is paired with the right user. The next layer happens between the card and the computer as the card authenticates itself to the computer's operating system with different information that the user does not even know, like the smartchip's unique ID (Something the card Is) and a symmetric Key (Something the card Knows).

In Chapter 10, I will reveal how you can create a Password Authentication Infrastructure with seven Levels of Assurance, without breaking the bank. When it comes to building the Chain of Trust, every single node and device should go through a separate layer of multi-factor authentication.

Network security must begin with authentication so you can know who is trying to get past your firewall. The more obstacles you can put up, the better. If you need more convincing, check out the next chapter for a comprehensive review of exactly how hackers go after your personal information, your company's proprietary information, your financials, and everything else you are storing on your servers!

CHAPTER 6

CYBER ATTACKS AND BEST DEFENSES

"Companies spend millions of dollars on firewalls, encryption, and secure access devices and it's money wasted because none of these measures address the weakest link in the security chain: the people who use, administer, operate and account for computer systems that contain protected information."

~ Kevin Mitnick, Hacker

The trick to security is not always trying to make it impossible to break. That is an almost futile endeavor. However, by putting up enough walls, in fact layers of walls, you can create a situation where the time it takes to crack your system will grow too long, the cost will become too expensive, and/or the resources needed to do it will be too rare to justify the value of the data they would acquire. It all eventually comes down to economics, for both the hacker and the CISO.

One should never under estimate the intelligence and resourcefulness of hackers. They think outside the box. They look for weak points to exploit that will lead them to another weak point, then another, and another, until they are in. Hackers don't care how they get in, just as long as they do. Sadly, most IT administrators don't think like hackers. IT administrators tend to think logically and sequentially, which is great for designing networks that allow companies and employees to do what they need to do. Hackers like to deconstruct a thing, then put it back together in a way that makes it do something it was never intended to do in the first place. It's a unique mindset, which makes them tough to stop and even tougher to catch.

To develop a strong cyber defense, business owners need to have a high-level understanding of what their CISO and IT managers guard against daily. Through this lens and understanding, risk assessments can be thoroughly analyzed so that the most appropriate security precautions for each environment can be implemented. 100% protection is usually cost-prohibitive. Because new ways of breaking into networks and files are being developed and released daily, it is impossible to stop every possible attack. I suggest you implement practical protection.

Common Password Attack Methods

The following is a comprehensive list of known attacks that hackers use to go after passwords. Knowing these attack methods helps determine your specific vulnerabilities and also helps justify your return on investment.

Brute-Force Attack:

A brute-force attack is the crudest, but sometimes the most effective way to break a password. It requires continuously trying every possible combination of letters, numbers, and special characters until a match is found. It does not require any injection of malware into the intended victim's computer or server.

Using a brute-force attack to go after Websites and servers is not always practical because many Websites and servers monitor for user names and passwords repeatedly being tried and failing to connect. After about six attempts, the account will be blocked and the user notified that there could be a problem.

The best defense against a brute-force attack is to make the time it takes to discover the password longer than the value of the information. This is easily accomplished by increasing the length, character mix, and randomness of the characters used to generate a password. A password manager will allow for long, constantly changing passwords that makes a brute-force attack virtually impossible.

Dictionary Attack:

The dictionary attack is a slight spinoff of the brute-force attack, but instead of trying every possible permutation, the hacker relies on the fact that humans generate passwords they can easily remember. This means passwords based on words found in a dictionary, names, dates, and keyboard patterns (e.g., 123456 or qwerty). Hackers actually create their own dictionary of the most commonly used passwords.

There are Websites that list the top 500 most commonly used passwords. Here are the top five reigning champs for the past 15 years:

- 123456
- password
- 12345678
- qwerty
- abc123

Any of those look familiar? The best defenses against dictionary attacks are password length, multiple character types, and character randomness. In other words, don't use passwords that spell actual words and don't use some easy keyboard pattern. The use of a password manager will make this easy on the user and completely eliminate the risk of this type of attack.

Over-the-Shoulder Surfers:

This used to be someone simply looking over your shoulder as you typed your password. However, with cameras being so small and available everywhere from smartphones, nanny cams, Google Glass, and closed-circuit cameras, over-the-shoulder attacks have become more anonymous and remote. The thief no longer has to stand next to you. A clever hacker could break into the video conferencing camera on your monitor and watch you typing.

The best defenses are common sense. Don't ever type your password while another person is standing next to you. If they are wearing Google Glasses, make them take them off or leave the room. If your computer has a video conferencing camera, then unplug it or get a lens cover. If you are in an environment where you have no control over the cameras present, then do your best to cover up the keyboard or pin pad with your hand, body, or something else so there is no clear view of your entry. With a password manager, no passwords are typed, so there is nothing for anyone to see.

Sticky Note Security:

Writing passwords on sticky notes and placing them in your office is not secure. Even trying to hide them under a tissue box or keyboard doesn't work because the odds are that someone can see you look at it.

Aside from the general insecurity of writing down passwords, thieves are actually paying for passwords to networks on the Internet black market. Disgruntled employees, cleaning crews, office visitors, or service people only need to take out their smartphone and snap a photo to capture your passwords and sell them online.

The main sticky note defense is to get employees out of the password management business. The only reasons passwords are written down are because people have too many, they are too complex, and they change too frequently to remember. A password manager removes the need to remember passwords.

Spamming, Phishing, and Pharming:

These are the most common tricks hackers use to get what they're after. They are also the most difficult attack strategy for IT to protect against, because they are directed at the human element using social engineering. If an employee believes they have received a legitimate email with an attachment or link, they will click on it. Many high profile cyber breaches started with a spam, phish, or pharm email attack, including Sony, JPMorgan Chase & Co., and Ashley Madison.

The best known email spamming scheme is the "Nigerian Scam" where a person informs you that their relative in a distant land has died and is worth millions of dollars. If you donate a little money to help this person recover their wealth, they will share the inheritance with you. Of course, you never see any of the money, and in many cases, the information you supply is enough for the cyberthief to quickly drain your savings and checking account balances down to zero.

You probably have seen emails that claim to be from your bank saying that there may be a problem with your account. In order to fix the problem you must click on the supplied link and enter your user name and password to authenticate yourself. This is a common phishing attack. Problem is, there is no problem with your account and you have just given a thief all he/she needs to know to steal all your money.

Emails that look like they absolutely came from people you know can be fraudulent. I once received an email from a good friend saying she was in Europe and her purse, passport, and all her money had been stolen. She begged me to send her money right away and she would pay me back when she got home. I checked. She was actually in her office a few miles away. I have also received an email from one of my own email accounts saying I was selling new Rolex watches. The funny thing is, I'm not in the business of selling watches.

Finally, pharming attacks occur via malware that covertly redirects you from a known Website to one that looks legitimate but is in fact bogus in an attempt to steal your log-on data. Make absolutely sure the URL is correct before entering any data.

All these and many more are examples of spamming, phishing, and pharming. And while each hoax is set up differently, what they all have in common is they link to sites that are designed by hackers to steal personal information and eventually all your money. While training and educating employees cannot completely stop an employee from replying to a bogus email or clicking an infected link, it can go a long way toward preventing behavior that could completely devastate an entire business.

The first line of defense is to question EVERY email before clicking on any attachment. Ask yourself, "Do I know this person and is this an attachment I'm expecting?" If there is even the slightest doubt, call the sender to confirm they sent it, or just delete it. Never, ever click on any links in any email until you are absolutely sure about it. It's also a good idea to view all emails in Preview before opening them. If it looks suspicious, it probably is. Delete it immediately.

Another defense is to verify that the link URL is correct. This can easily be done by hovering the mouse pointer over a link to determine if the address looks correct. Better yet, open a new browser window, do a Web search for the company and click on that link.

Finally, use a good password manager. No matter how a link is presented in an email or message, a secure password manager will compare the link address with the one it stores. If they don't match, then the password is never entered or transmitted.

Spear Phishing:

While similar to the phishing emails discussed above, spear phishing is a little more sophisticated and targeted. The email you receive looks like it came from a known business associate or boss. These emails often include file attachments, links, or requests for sensitive company information.

Hackers use spear phishing as part of their social engineering attacks because they know that employees really want to be helpful and rarely question any requests that come from upper management. In today's world of cyber breaches, management needs to have a policy that allows employees to ask for confirmation if something looks odd, and thank them when they do.

As mentioned before, question anything that looks odd, and hover the mouse over any links to view the URL. If it looks suspicious, then don't click it. And if you really are not sure, send a separate new email, or better yet, call the sender to confirm that they sent the email. Password managers protect your log-on site links.

Malware and Keyloggers:

Malicious software (malware) are programs that get loaded onto a computer or network with the intent to monitor, steal, or disrupt data. There are numerous ways that these programs can infect a computer. The most common way is through bogus email attachments, infected software applications, and corrupted Websites. Malware attacks are designed to put an entire network at risk.

A keylogger is a particular type of malware that records everything typed by a user. The information is stored on a hidden file periodically sent to the hacker. The hacker then looks through the file to find accounts, user names, passwords, credit card numbers, Social Security numbers, and anything else they deem valuable.

While anti-virus and anti-malware programs can help protect a system from these programs, they can only protect against known vulnerabilities. New malware programs and variations of older programs are released daily, making it impossible for any anti-virus software to catch everything. Every time a new virus is released, security software will become useless until that virus is discovered, added to the anti-virus software, and you have installed the update.

When it comes to password security, the best way to prevent a keylogger from discovering your passwords is to never type them. A good password manager will implement auto-form fills and keyboard emulations so the end-user never has to type a password. Password files, or their hash valuation, are stored in computers and server databases. These files need to be securely encrypted, hashed, and salted. This way, any data that is stolen is useless.

Storing Passwords in the Browser:

This is one of the early ways software companies tried to make password management easier on the user. Note that I said "easier," not "safer." The browser file that stores passwords is well known to hackers. All they need to do is steal the file and then have their computer run programs to break any encryption or protections.

Another problem with passwords in browsers is that they do not authenticate users before logging them in. When you walk away from your computer and leave it running, there is nothing to stop someone else from going to your computer, clicking a Website in your favorites file, and then have your computer automatically log them into your bank account, for example.

The defense here is, do not use Web browser storage. Second, don't leave computers unlocked and unattended. The best defense is to use a multi-factor authentication password manager.

Unencrypted Email Intercepts:

Have you ever sent someone a user name and password via an email? Have you ever received a forgotten user name and password via email? Were those emails secure?

If you are like most of us, you probably answered "Yes" to the first two questions and "No" to the last. Hackers know how to intercept email traffic. They may get your emails by hacking the sender's computer, your computer, or any number of servers the email passes through before it gets to its destination.

Programs like Outlook can send encrypted email. All you need to do is purchase a certificate and Public/Private Key pair. An alternative solution is to subscribe to one of many secure email services. These services ensure that all email traffic is encrypted so that only authorized recipients are allowed to read them. The interesting conundrum occurs when you ask yourself, "How do you log into these services?" Most likely, you need a user name and password. How secure is that password and its management? When implementing cybersecurity, the entire chain of events needs to be analyzed, not just one or two components.

Rainbow Table Attack:

A Rainbow Table is just a dictionary or table that has been optimized to crack password hashes. It's a variation of a Pass the Hash attack. A hacker will steal a password data file that has been hashed. Usually, every password within the data file has been hashed using the same hash function and seed. Similar to a brute-force attack, the Rainbow Table tries every known hash value that is stored to find the correct one.

How does the cyberthief know he has the correct seed value? That's where the list of the most common passwords comes into play. If the hash reveals the same valuation as some of the most common passwords, then the hash seed value is correct.

The defense against a Rainbow Table attack involves securing the data files and using better hash functions. One way to scramble the hash value is to run another hash on the original hash valuation. This increases the security because the hacker will not know the number of times the file was hashed separately, and the hacker may be missing one of the hash values in their table.

The second defense is called "Salting." This makes it very difficult for the hacker to really know that he has the correct password. Another way to add even more complexity is to have one of the hash seeds tied to a user's smartcard or token. Now, even the institution storing your passwords will not be able to reverse them, since they don't have your token. A strong, multi-factor authentication password manager will easily accomplish this.

Social Engineering:

When hackers use psychology to make people reveal information that they would not otherwise reveal, that is social engineering. This type of hack might come as a phone call from what sounds like a legitimate organization asking you to verify some information. Or, someone looking and acting like an IT administrator could appear and ask for your password to resolve an issue.

Companies need to train and regularly remind employees that they must never reveal or share their password with anyone, no matter who they say they are or why they need it. To insure that employees don't do this, you can set up your system so they never even know their passwords. A smartcard based Password Authentication Infrastructure solution makes that possible since it ties into Active Directory. If an employee has no way of knowing his password, then there is nothing he can disclose.

Good Samaritan Attack:

Crackers have been known to intentionally drop a thumb drive in a company's parking lot or lobby they would like to hack or harm. They know that some nice employee will come along, pick it up, take it to their desk, and plug it in so they can find out who it belongs to and return it. This form of social engineering has unleashed many problems into computers and networks. The thumb drive actually contains malware that gets uploaded into the company's network. Once the network is infected, the hacker can go after password files, sensitive information, set themselves up as a super administrator, or simply release more destructive viruses like Ransomware. Again, employees need to be trained to never insert found devices into their computers. They should turn the drive over to IT who may be able to look at the contents safely, or just throw it away.

Advanced Persistent Threats (APT):

Businesses, organizations, and government agencies are the typical targets of APT attacks. These attacks are perpetrated by very skilled, covert crackers who meticulously attack one cybersecurity defense barrier after another. Often it takes one seemingly innocent mistake (like the Good Samaritan Attack) that the cracker exploits. Once in, their malware will monitor activities and gather vital network information to then crack the next defensive barrier.

These attacks can take time to fully implement, and often go completely unde-tected by IT administrators. Anti-malware and anti-virus software offer little to no protection. The attacks look like normal traffic noise. Once the hacker is in, then he can add his credentials into the network, look like any other IT administrator, and do whatever he wants to data, peripheral devices, or military equipment. New defensive measures are being used to neutralize this kind of attack.

The covert nature of these attacks and attackers is why many data breaches go undetected for over 200 days. Typically, what tips IT off is when their systems start falling apart, and all hell breaks loose.

Remote Administrator Tools (RAT) :

A Remote Administration Tool is a great tool for tech support. RATs are used to help fix computer and software problems on remote machines through the Internet. If you have ever called tech support and had them take control of your computer to fix a problem, they used a RAT.

The problem of course is when a RAT is used for illegitimate reasons. Once a system is breached, a RAT allows a hacker to work in the background, hidden from both the IT Administrator and the end-user. From this stealth position, hackers can monitor activity, manage files, install additional software, control the entire system, change essential settings, manipulate certificates, and so much more.

RATs become a password concern because of their ability to monitor the typing of passwords, capture keystrokes, access password files, change passwords, and everything else a system administrator can do. Of course, you know I'm going to ask the question... Is this a password problem or a system problem?

The best way to protect against a RAT is by always verifying that the person or entity requesting access is authorized. There are two important ways to do that. First, employees should be trained (and empowered to act appropriately) when an unknown person claims to be a service tech, they should contact IT to make sure that person is authorized. And second, to prevent RATs from getting passwords by way of cyber tricks, it is the responsibility of management and IT to remove the employee from the role of managing passwords.

Cross-Site Scripting (XSS):

Cross-site scripting (XSS) happens when malicious code is injected into dynamic Web pages. XSS modifies the settings or variables within the Webpage's database.

The hacker must first attack and compromise a Website. Once access is accomplished, they download their malicious code into the Webpage's source code. For example, some Web plugin programs commonly found in WordPress and Joomla! require permission to access resources from another client or network computer. XSS injects malicious scripts written in JavaScript, VBScript, ActiveX, HTML, or Flash to grant those same permissions to an unauthorized third party (the hacker).

Thereafter, when a visitor goes to the Website, the malware is typically injected into the visitor's computer by way of Login forms, Forgotten Password forms, and Credit Card Processing forms.

By injecting malicious XSS scripts into Web pages, an attacker can gain elevated access privileges to private information, intercept user input, place cookies, display false pop-up reminders to update an application, and a variety of other browser services.

Cross-site scripting is a network security problem where hackers capture password data, not a password authentication problem. Some of the defenses include validating input to dynamic Web pages, installing strong name-brand security monitoring tools, and getting rid of this belief that you are too small for anyone to notice so you don't need security. Face it, you are doing everything you can to get customers to notice you. What makes you think hackers don't see you?

Lumping All Data Together:

In this chapter, you've learned many of the ways hackers break passwords. Almost all these attacks rely on the poor management of passwords or the password data file. Now, let's shift focus and talk about the security around how password data files are stored.

When it comes to security, not all data are the same. Some data are intended for the general public, some are intended for employees, and some are very sensitive and intended for only select groups or upper management.

Back when I was working for a military defense contractor, we categorized documents as "Unclassified," "Confidential," "Secret," "Top Secret," and "Core Secret." All data first need to be assigned a security level. That level then determines the way that data are both stored and transported. Password data files need to be given Top Secret or Core Secret classifications allowing them to be easily segregated and assigned appropriate security procedures.

In the commercial world, both unclassified and top secret data are unfortunately often lumped together on the same server. If you have one server storing blog posts alongside research and development, financial data, and password data files, you are literally asking for trouble. Hackers target the weakest points within a network and then snake their way through to your sensitive information. When a company treats all data equally, it creates a monumental problem for the IT administrator who tries to monitor everything. Expecting IT to monitor everything is, at best, inefficient. The better solution is for IT to concentrate monitoring on the important information. Segregating that data makes the task much easier and the data much more secure.

Companies may not need as many different clearance levels as the military, but the concept is sound. Blogs, press releases, and product data sheets are open to the public and require less monitoring. Inter-office emails, schedules, and similar data should be classified as secured for internal use only. Financials, HR, R&D, Password Files, and Customer Personal Information should be classified as very sensitive, with the highest protections.

Here are a few simple practices to eliminate this vulnerability:

- Classify data according to sensitivity.

- Have separate servers store information based on sensitivity.

- Put greater security protections on servers with more sensitive data.

- Do not allow one server to directly communicate with another, where the hacker can use it as a bridge.

Other Attacks:

There are Zero-Day (0-day) viruses, Distributed Denial of Service (DDoS) attacks, and many more that target processes other than authentication. Attacks are launched against Windows, Linux, OS-X, Android, and other operating systems. Some attacks are old and are being revived. Others are just a slight permutation of a known attack. And some are completely new. New attacks and mutated older attacks are constantly hitting the Web. Cybersecurity is not just about the number of different attacks but the volume of attacks slamming a company's network daily. It's very difficult for IT administrators to stay current because they have the more important role of just keeping the network running and employees connected. This leaves very little time to fully monitor all activities.

IT relies on software monitoring tools to alert them when something does not look right. The problem is that these alerts are only as good as the capabilities of the software. Plus, when these monitoring tools are used on servers that store both sensitive and non-sensitive information, the sheer volume of data to analyze often overwhelms IT. This is one reason why the average time for IT to discover a breach is over 200 days.

According to the *Symantec Internet Security Threat Report, April 2015*, crypto-ransomware attacks were up to 8.8 million victims in 2014. Large businesses saw over 67% of all spear-phishing attacks followed by small businesses of less than 250 employees with nearly 20% of the reported attacks. Most of these attacks are automated, making employees (and their companies) vulnerable to the "one in every 208 emails" reported to contain malware.

The goals and resources of hackers vary depending on who is sponsoring the attack: Nation States, Organized Crime, Hacktivists, disgruntled employees, or Script Kiddies. There is no one attack that reveals everything and there is no one defense that offers 100% protection.

Home businesses and small- to medium-size businesses are prime targets. With so many non-technical people creating Websites using tools like WordPress, Joomla!, or other Web page building tools, security is rarely a top concern. These site owners often think they are too small for a hacker to target. Wrong. SMBs are exactly who hackers want to target because they know passwords are typically weak, there is little to no site monitoring, and security is either absent or using some cheap product from an unknown developer. Once the Website is infected, their visitors' computers become infected simply by accessing their account. From there, the propagation spreads.

While news reports focus on the "weakness" of passwords, they fail to discuss how the hackers actually get in. It's understandable that the media would spotlight passwords because they are a common source of frustration for virtually everyone who owns a device that connects them with the world. Unfortunately, that sensationalized focus diverts attention from the deeper discussion about secure authentication.

The threats and ramifications of a data breach have become so severe that large corporations are now imposing cybersecurity requirements on their suppliers and vendors. If a SMB does not secure its network to the level a corporation requires, they will drop that supplier. So ask yourself, how would losing a Boeing, Proctor and Gamble, or General Motors affect your business?

CHAPTER 7

PKI: A LOCK IS ONLY AS SECURE AS ITS KEY

"It is important to realize that any lock can be picked with a big enough hammer."

~ Sun Systems and Network Administrator Manual

When it comes to security implementations, there is a big difference between the theoretical and the practical. In the theoretical world, all algorithms work flawlessly. There are no infrastructure vulnerabilities, and security protects against every attack. In the practical world, things do not always go as planned.

In the real world, new vulnerabilities raise their ugly heads from places no one ever anticipated. The realization that Certificate Authorities (CA), certificates, and Private Keys can be compromised rocks the foundation of asymmetric ciphers and cybersecurity. Once the Private Key is compromised (something security pundits believe is nearly impossible), just like with a password, cybersecurity goes out the window. That's because IT cannot differentiate between a hacker and a legitimate employee if the correct credentials are presented. The more complex the system, the more attack points there are to exploit. The more complex the system, the more installation mistakes IT can make. The more complex the system, the more details there are to manage. And, you would be hard pressed to find a more complex system than PKI.

Threats to PKI

The purpose of this book is to help the reader understand how to make password authentication secure. To accomplish this goal, I need to explain how other security authentication solutions are attacked and the ways engineers try to block those attacks. These solutions go to great lengths to protect their Keys, which makes analyzing them a great source of ideas for protecting passwords.

Cryptographic Keys and digital certificates are always offered up as being far better and more secure than lowly passwords. But, they may not be as secure as previously touted. Let's take a closer look.

In a recent *Ponemon Research: 2015 Cost of Failed Trust Report,* it states:

> After weathering a rising tide of attacks and vulnerabilities, the *2015 Cost of Failed Trust Report* research shows the digital trust that underpins most of the world's economy is nearing its breaking point, and there is no replacement in sight. This research found that thousands of IT security professionals believe that, over the next two years, the risk facing every Global 5000 company from attacks on Keys and certificates is at least $53M. This is up 51% from the risk estimated in 2013. And for four years running, all of the organizations surveyed have responded to multiple attacks on Keys and certificates.
>
> Security professionals rank a *Cryptoapocalypse*-like event, a scenario where the standard algorithms of trust like RSA and SHA are compromised and exploited overnight, as the most alarming threat. But lurking close behind in second place is the misuse of certificates used for enterprise mobility with applications like WiFi, VPN, and MDM/EMM.

The more complex the infrastructure becomes, the greater the chance for human and computer errors and mistakes. So before you make an expensive and complex leap into certificate-based authentication, here are a few of the known problems and attacks...at least the ones that have been made public.

What "They" Are Not Telling You

Most people don't know that companies that issue certificates and Keys use passwords to secure them. If you forget or lose your password, then you lose your certificate and must buy a new one.

Certificates and Keys have brought serious complexity to network security. They require special Key generators, Certificate Authorities, Registration Authority, Validation Authentication, Revocation lists, cryptographic accelerators, and more. Complexity tends to create confusion, unknown parts, and mistakes. Keys are often mismanaged at best and, at worst, completely un-managed. The average corporation employing PKI has over 20,000 different cipher Keys and certificates, and over 50% of those corporations' IT administrators don't know where all the Keys are located within the network. This lack of knowledge allows hackers to easily inject their own certificates into networks, undetected by IT.

In all the latest high profile breaches, the attacks went undetected for more than 200 days. That's over six months! Why does this happen?

Most protection protocols can only protect against known attacks. They are useless against anything unknown. As hackers mutate different attacks, they essentially create undetectable variations. So, unless IT happens to accidently stumble upon something unusual or their protection software got an update with the correct detections, hackers get to play inside the network for as long as they want.

Certificate supporters suggest that Key length, Key-protecting hardware, and no secret sharing is why certificates are better than passwords. But there is no reason from the computer's standpoint that passwords can't be as long as or even longer than any Key. There is some Key sharing required (e.g., Symmetric Keys), but the same hardware used to protect Private keys is just as capable of protecting passwords. Remember, it's all the same to the computer. If Keys and certificates are so secure, why did the Intel Security report warn that certificate-based malware has increased by 700% in the last four years (2012-2015)?

Finally, once a certificate has been issued, it cannot be transferred or recovered and it certainly can't be changed as frequently as a password without additional costs and overhead issues. IT has the ability to create and implement a policy where passwords change every 30, 60, or 90 days. The cost to change a password is basically zero. A certificate typically stays the same for three years, and if compromised, then another certificate has to be requested for an additional fee. Depending on the type of certificate, it can cost from $30 to $150 per each user.

For PKI to work, *every* technology component, *every* service company, and *every* communications channel has to be secure. So let's review the PKI system and show some examples where hackers exploited various infrastructure weaknesses and mistakes.

Can You Trust the Certificate Authority?

First, look at the process of obtaining a digital certification. The certificate begins at the Registration Authority (RA) and Certificate Authority (CA). For two companies or agencies to securely communicate and trust each other, they first have to trust the same certificate-issuing company. While there can be different hierarchal levels and locations of CAs, eventually a single entity, or trusted third-party, validates all the lower-level CAs.

An employee will submit a request to the IT administrator for a digital certificate. The IT administrator contacts the familiar RA and submits all the required documentation (like the employee's driver's license, birth certificate and/or passport) to verify the identity of the employee. After reviewing and approving all the documents, the RA submits a request for certificate from a CA. Once reviewed, the CA takes the personal information supplied by the RA and issues a certificate and frequently the Public/Private Key pair as well.

This process seems simple and should be error-free, but it only takes one successful exploitation to break the trust chain. As the following story highlights, security is only as good as the infrastructure.

⚏ SOMETHING TO THINK ABOUT

On July 19, 2011 DigiNotar, a Dutch digital certificate authority (CA), confirmed it was breached and several dozen fraudulent digital certificates were issued. Earlier in 2015, Comodo Group, Inc. warned that it too had issued fraudulent certificates. It is surmised that the hacker impersonated a Registration Authority to request the certificates. These fraudulent certificates affected the operating systems, applications, and browsers of such industry giants as Google, Microsoft, Yahoo, Mozilla, and others.

How the attacker actually fooled the CA is still under investigation, but one possible explanation starts with the use of an individual's stolen personal information from identity theft. The hacker submits the stolen personal information to the CA and requests a certificate. When the CA checks the identity theft victim's background, all the information looks legitimate, so a certificate is issued. This example also highlights that identity theft is so much more than having your credit card number stolen.

On the Internet, personal information (also called "credentials") is used to create a trail of seemingly legitimate information. This trail creates "breeder documents" to start more advanced hacks into more important networks. Next, the theft of unsecured passwords also allows hackers to change an individual's profile information and re-route notices without the user's knowledge. The reason I bring up these two points is to help you understand the degree to which hackers go to break into networks.

Without too much technical jargon, fake certificates allow man-in-the-middle attacks to occur. The attacker can intercept, read, and alter correspondences. Software patches and updates might be intercepted and then infected with malware before being passed on. Web browsers can inject any code into any network in a trusted manner, all without the user's knowledge. Don't we always trust that security patch or software update from a trusted vendor?

To mitigate the damage, DigiNotar and other companies claim that the fake certificates have been revoked, but revocation isn't a sure thing. The rogue certificates could be used for one-off targeted attacks, and therefore would be tough to pinpoint. Even with these notices, companies are dependent on browser updates for full protection. If a fraudulent certificate and malware are inserted into an application, plug-in, or driver update, it's not too much of a stretch to ask if the malware could have blocked the actual revocation cleanup. It's also unsure if every rogue certificate was discovered.

CA-issued certificates are at the heart of Secure Socket Layer (SSL) and PKI security. These certificates create a chain of trust back to the certificate authority's root certificate. The security and implementation of certificates is only as good as the root's security. If the root is compromised, all of the issued certificates are, in turn, also compromised.

⚏ SOMETHING TO THINK ABOUT

One of the components that allowed Stuxnet to infiltrate the Iranian nuclear enrichment system in 2010 was the use of what Windows thought was a valid certificate. This certificate weakness example demonstrates an administrative problem and not whether certificate-based systems offer viable authentication. That is not dissimilar from improperly administering password security.

The certificate process is only as viable as the verification process of the individual and as secure as the CA operation. In the past, many CAs simply used a person's email address, and credit card number to identify the individual. A good

RA/CA requires driver's license, birth certificate, passport, and additional trusted third party verifications. Fake driver's licenses, birth certificates, and stolen Social Security numbers put the validity of many documents into question. If a company wants to accept a certificate, it first must trust that the certificate authority did its due diligence in vetting every individual.

The process is not flawed, but often the management of the infrastructure is. In this first stage, you have to trust the individual, their documents, the Registration Authority (RA), and Certificate Authority (CA). A company can either spend time and money reviewing the entire verification process (assuming they have the resources and knowledge to do so,) or just blindly trust it.

Where to Keep Your Keys

After the verification is complete and a certificate is created, the next phase is the Public/Private Key generation and secure Private Key storage. Where and how a Private Key is stored determines the security and trust of the entire certificate system. Debbie Deutsch and Beth Cohen in their June 17, 2003 eSecurityPlanet. com article, *"Public Key Infrastructure: Invisibly Protecting Your Digital Assets,"* summed up the security of the Private Key as follows:

> PKI operation depends on protecting the Private Keys. Sometimes keys are generated by a computer and stored in memory and on disk. This is acceptable for everyday security. However, it is possible for someone to break into the computer—perhaps in person, perhaps over a network—and retrieve the Private Key. As a result, very sensitive information or resources need greater protection. Specialized hardware peripheral devices can provide stronger security by generating Keys, signing, and decrypting information, so the Private Key never leaves the device. Protecting the Key then becomes a matter of protecting the device from unauthorized use. It may be carried by its owner, locked up, password protected, etc.

⊞ SOMETHING TO THINK ABOUT

Cloudflare, a popular off-site storage hosting service, launched "The Heartbleed Challenge" on April 11, 2014. They tasked the hacking community to use the "Heartbleed" virus to steal the private Secure Socket Layer (SSL) Keys off their servers running the Open SSL framework. The results of the challenge surprised even Cloudflare.

Nine hours later, software engineers Fedor Indutny and Ilkka Mattila at NCSC-FI had obtained the server's Private Keys. Cloudflare announced that it is possible to expose the SSL private encryption Keys. Both Indutny and Mattila sent numerous pings (2.5 million and 100,000 respectively) requesting the Private Key. The next day, two other hackers were able to get in. It seems that when a server reboots, there is a period of time when these keys are vulnerable, and Cloudflare rebooted the server about six hours into the challenge.

The implications of retrieving an SSL Private Key are significant. In cyber-security: anyone possessing a compromised SSL Private Key can use it to host an impostor site that is virtually impossible to detect. The same https prefix and padlock icon accompanying the site's authentic server would appear, giving the visitor a false sense of security.

The challenge showed that there is an SSL Private Key vulnerability, even when a specially prepared server was configured for the test and monitored by IT administrators aware that their servers were going to be attacked. If hackers were able to penetrate a closely monitored server, how does a company with limited IT resources focused on daily network operations and resetting forgotten passwords expect to secure their Keys?

The recommended fix was to revoke and replace the old certificates as soon as possible because the compromised Private Keys can continue to be used to access user data. This is a good suggestion, but doesn't take into account the time and cost to a business to do this. Changing Keys is not as simple as changing passwords.

> "If every site revoked its certificates, it would impose a significant burden and performance penalty on the Internet," wrote Nick Sullivan, Security Engineer at CloudFlare in a blog post. "At CloudFlare the scale of the reissuance and revocation process could break the CA [Certificate Authority] infrastructure."

A new certificate means a new Key pair. Information that was encrypted with an old Key cannot be decrypted by the new Key. This forces companies to keep both Keys, which further increase vulnerability. A companywide recommendation that everyone change passwords would be useless if the company did not first change certificates because the hackers would see the new passwords, too.

Ms. Deutsch and Ms. Cohen have shown there is a PKI hierarchy of storage options based on the sensitivity of information. Choosing between software based Private Keys versus hardware Private Keys is determined by that data sensitivity.

I am making the same argument for a secure password manager. Passwords and PKI are not competing; rather, they are complementary. How and where you want to use both is based on a threat/risk assessment. For example, do the employees on the loading docks need an expensive hardware-based PKI solution to enter shipping information? Or would a secure password manager sufficiently manage the risks at a fraction of the cost?

The complexity of computer networks for even something as simple as powering up a server could be a source of either human or machine errors. These errors are not an indictment of the effectiveness or value of authentication methodologies like passwords or PKI, but rather a reminder about how clever hackers can be and that security can never be taken for granted.

How Much is Security Worth?

A more secure and usually more expensive Private Key protection method is the Hardware Security Module (HSM) or Trusted Platform Module (TPM). These are physical security devices installed within a locked server room that is protected from unauthorized access. To rank the security level a device offers, the computer industry has adopted an industry standard known as the Common Criteria (CC) Evaluation Assurance Level (EAL). When tested, the higher numerical valuation a device achieves, the stronger the security. The sensitivity and classification of information a company is protecting will determine the appropriate level of HSM device to install. Of course, the higher the level of certification, the greater the cost of the HSM. When data is properly classified and segmented, the appropriate HSM can insure a company is not over- or under-protecting their data. Typically, CC EAL 4+, 5+, or 6+ are used for an HSM device.

In researching the security threats on HSMs, I found 2006 and 2009 articles about PIN vulnerabilities attributed to hacking an HSM. While the following case in point may be a few years old, it does highlight why HSM devices are advertised as "attack resistant" and not "attack proof." The vulnerability can lie outside the technology.

⚏ SOMETHING TO THINK ABOUT

When a customer pays for a purchase with an ATM or Debit card, they type in a PIN. PINs are supposed to be encrypted in transit, which should theoretically protect them if someone intercepts the data. The problem, however, is that a PIN must pass through multiple HSMs across multiple bank networks before it reaches the customer's bank. At every switching point, the PIN must be decrypted, then re-encrypted with the proper Key for its next leg in its journey. The security of the entire process depends on by whom and how well these HSMs are configured and managed. The most common method criminals are using to get the PIN numbers is to trick the application programming interface (or API) of the hardware security module (HSM) into providing the encryption key. This is possible due to poor configuration of the HSM or vulnerabilities created from having bloated functions on the device.

Another vulnerability occurs when the HSM communicates with the issuing bank's mainframe to process the transaction. Here the PIN and the customer's 16-digit account number are briefly held unencrypted in the mainframe's system memory waiting for authorization of the transaction. It is here that hackers use "scraper" malware to capture the data. It is estimated that as much as a third of all PIN theft cases involve scrapers.

In a Cambridge University paper published in 2003, a researcher presented how attacks, with the help of an insider, would yield PINs from an issuer bank's system. Then in 2006, two Israeli computer security researchers devised a much more sophisticated attack that also required the assistance of an insider. With access to the HSM and the API, knowledge of the HSM configuration, and knowledge of the network's architecture, it is possible for a hacker to acquire bank PINs.

Brian Phelps, Director of Program Services for Thales Group, emphasizes that the problem is how systems are configured and managed. "It's a very difficult challenge to protect against the lazy administrator," Mr. Phelps said. "Out of the box, the HSMs come configured in a very secure fashion if customers just deploy them as is. But for many operational reasons, customers choose to alter those default security configurations—supporting legacy applications may be one example—which creates the vulnerabilities."

As the vulnerabilities to HSM devices rises, the PCI Security Standards Council has been at the forefront in testing, issuing industry standards, and enforcing physical and logical requirements for the protection of sensitive data. While PINs may never be 100% secure, organizations like the PCI Security Standards Council offer the industry a high level of assurance. Companies should only purchase products that have gone through the PCI Council certification.

IT administrators and engineers can make the technology safe, but weak OS security, a bad Web request front end, or a rogue admin can thwart even the best controls.

Don't Change the Key, Change the Lock

Smartcards are also used to generate and store Private Keys. Because of their mobility, they offer a good alternative to a server-based HSM. The processing power and security mechanisms deployed keep the Private Key in a very controlled container. Some smartcards can even generate their own Key pair internally, thus never allowing the Private Key out of its secure container. Or so it seems. Even with advances in smartcard technologies, hackers still find system vulnerabilities in obscure areas.

⚏ SOMETHING TO THINK ABOUT

When the Sykipot, a zero-day Trojan, was combined with a keylogger malware, thieves were able to steal a smartcard's PIN and read the stored certificate. While the smartcard was never actually cracked, Sykipot capitalized on a weakness found in the computer's operation system and applications that allowed the hacker to take control of the smartcard as if he were the owner.

The U.S. Department of Defense (DoD) uses one of the most advanced and expensive PC/SC x.509 deployed multi-factor smartcard infrastructures to date. In 2011, the DoD claimed that Chinese hackers infected their computers with the Sykipot virus and stole the PIN numbers of many government employees' smartcards. With these PINs, the hackers were able to use the stored certificates to access files and networks. The DoD has yet to publicly disclose what information was accessed or the sensitivity of the data.

In an attack like this, the user is unaware of the compromise. While this is not a direct attack on the smartcard, it is an attack on the infrastructure. In an online article, Jaime Blasco, Director of AlienVault Labs, offered his solution: "One way is to add another layer of authentication, such as a one-time password."

Am I the only one who sees the irony here? Is he saying that the best way to protect against the Sykipot attack of a certificate is with a **PASSWORD?** This was at the same time that White House Cybersecurity Coordinator Michael Daniel stated, "I often say that one of my key goals in my job that I would really love to be able to do is to kill the password dead."

Just to be clear, these attacks had nothing to do with theoretical aspects of PKI, but rather hackers exploiting flaws in operating systems, operations, and peripheral components that lead to the certificate. In other words, they attacked the infrastructure. Passwords and Private Keys are only as secure as the infrastructure protecting them. And insiders are a major threat to protecting sensitive information.

Surrender Your Private Keys By Order of a Judge

There is a key recovery recommendation to address lost or forgotten Private Keys, or when an employee leaves the company and their encrypted emails and documents need to be recovered. It is known as "Key Escrowing."

Key escrowing is a proactive means by which a Private Key is first split into two parts, then one half is stored by an outside trusted escrow service, and the other half by a government agency. Supposedly, only under carefully controlled circumstances, like a court order, can law enforcement put the two parts together. However, with some of the recent reports of government spying on citizens, hacks into major corporations, and nation-sanctioned cyber espionage, one has to be concerned if legal safeguards and protections are strong enough to protect Private Keys.

Remember the introduction of the "clipper chip" back in 1993? Manufacturers were being required to place this chip in phones, computers, and any other type of communications device. The controversy was about having a backdoor cryptographic key stored in an escrow account. After a government agency "established their authority" to monitor a suspect's communication, then the Key would be surrendered to that government agency. Many privacy advocacy groups who monitor unlawful surveillance were in an uproar, fearing citizens would be subjected to increased and possibly illegal government surveillance. By 1996, the clipper chip was no longer relevant, mainly due to widespread encryption tools like Pretty Good Privacy (PGP) and the chip's poor security protocols. However, the U.S. government continues to press for Key escrow.

Following the Snowden disclosures, Apple and Google announced in September 2014 that their new smartphones would include unbreakable encryption features to protect stored data. This new direction prompted strong reactions from different law enforcement authorities. Former Attorney General Eric H. Holder, Jr. said this could imperil investigations in kidnapping and other cases. FBI Director James B. Comey asked, why would companies "market something expressly to allow people to place themselves beyond the law." Suggestions are being made for another backdoor that would require a special key to unlock the data only after a warrant has been issued.

⚏ SOMETHING TO THINK ABOUT

I recently came across a case in July, 2013 where the United States Department of Justice (DOJ) demanded, and then subpoenaed, a privately held company, Lavabit LLC, surrender the private encryption keys of their 410,000 customers. What is particularly disconcerting about the Lavabit case is that the DOJ believes that it can take away the privacy of innocent civilians in order to investigate one nefarious suspect.

Putting the privacy rights argument aside, there is a vulnerability with the security of Private Keys. The logic follows that a subpoena assumes that an IT administrator has the ability to gain access to the Private Keys. Access confirms that the Private Keys are vulnerable. Since the Keys are vulnerable, they will be targeted by hackers, organized crime, nation-states, hacktivists, and others. If they are targeted, they are susceptible to compromise. If compromised, the security of that PKI installation is destroyed. If the PKI installation is destroyed, untold damages and costs could be incurred with lost R&D, manipulation of data, technology replacement costs, and more. Those costs may be too high for a company to bear. High recovery and legal costs can lead to bankruptcy and employee layoffs.

While there are very good reasons why the "good guys" feel they need to request and recover Private Keys, those same permissions can be exploited.

The goal of this chapter is not to undermine or discredit the viability of PKI and network security, but rather to prove the old security adage, "Anything created by man can eventually be broken by man, given enough time, money, and resources."

PKI offers many advantages in authenticating and securing data. However, it must be implemented correctly and the entire system must constantly be reviewed and tested for flaws and vulnerabilities. And from what we have seen in many of the stories above, the hacker first gains access through seemingly unrelated avenues. A simple operating system patch update, a new device connected to an outside network, or some bought-off employee may be all it takes.

Passwords also have their flaws and vulnerabilities, but like the PKI issues discussed above, you do not abandon a strong, security model because of a few discovered vulnerabilities. Rather, you fix and strengthen the security. When passwords are given the same level of resources as Private Keys, they too will be secure.

CHAPTER 8

CYBER AUTHENTICATION INFRASTRUCTURES

"Security is a process, not a product."

~ Bruce Schneier

Building an infrastructure is not easy. Computer infrastructures are system-wide solutions, requiring industry and government standards, software, hardware, network topographies, communication protocols, and a number of other pieces that all must operate together to make its usage seamless to the user. With the rash of data breaches, network attacks, and compromised confidential data occurring every day, security is now an important component of every computer infrastructure.

Cybersecurity requires many different safeguards, but the very first safeguard has to be Cyber Authentication. Authentication ensures that only users with authorized access privileges are allowed in and all the rest are kept out.

Cybersecurity infrastructure is designed to deliver five trust elements:

- **Authentication** – The person or machine is in fact who they claim to be.

- **Authorization** – A person or machine is approved to access another machine or computer network and the data in it.

- **Non-repudiation** – Undisputable verification that only a specific person or machine could have performed a specific action.

- **Data integrity** – The information sent is exactly the information received.

- **Signature** – Securely signing online documents by combining authentication, non-repudiation, and data integrity.

Cyber authentication infrastructure utilizes the first three elements: Authentication, Authorization, and Non-repudiation.

With all the data breaches these last few years, the computer industry is aggressively proposing and developing new cyber authentication solutions. Some of the proposals include Kerberos, Federated Identity Management, OpenID Connect, and Identity Assurance (IDA). Currently, none of these proposals has achieved full industry adoption or deployment. Their biggest hurdle is building and implementing an infrastructure.

As these proposals are still developing, it makes more sense to discuss the four widely accepted and currently deployed cybersecurity infrastructures: Public Key Infrastructure (PKI), Symmetric Key Infrastructure (SKI), One Time Passwords (OTP), and Single Sign-On (SSO). I am also introducing a fifth option: Password Authentication Infrastructure (PAI).

When it comes to choosing and deploying the correct cyber authentication infrastructure for your business or organization, you want to match your needs to the technology. What is often overlooked is that these infrastructures are not mutually exclusive. Don't get caught in the trap that one authentication fits all—it doesn't. A network can have more than one way to authenticate a person. At a minimum, you will want to take into account the person's level of trust and authorization rights, your budget constraints, ongoing cost of ownership, and time to deploy.

A typical organizational hierarchy consists of 10% upper management, 30% mid-level management, with the remaining 60% being employees. When the responsibilities of these three groups are analyzed, PKI, SKI, and PAI are appropriate for the top tier, SKI and PAI for the middle tier, and PAI for the bottom tier. There is no need to allocate the highest cost solution for the 90% of your employees who will only use 10% of the available features. To figure out which infrastructure is right for your organization, I will break down the strengths and weaknesses of each.

Public Key Infrastructure

Public Key Infrastructure (PKI) is deployed when an unlimited number of unknown users require authentication into an unlimited number of managed networks. It is the most widely used of all the certificate-based authentication infrastructures. Ironically, most applications and Web-based services cannot support certificates for authentication. Therefore, PKI authentication typically entails connecting into a server's Lightweight Directory Access Protocol (LDAP), like the familiar Microsoft Windows Active Directory. Active Directory then manages the User Names and Passwords to all the authorized applications, clouds, and servers. In other words, PKI uses certificates and multi-factor authentication at the frontend (Active Directory) to manage password log-on into everything else.

PKI, of course, does more than just authentication. It is also used for secure information transfer, to create legally binding Internet contracts, and to give assurances that only the authorized individual performed a task on the network. PKI leverages multi-factor authentication, symmetric cipher, asymmetric cipher, hash functions, and HSM to offer five trust elements:

- **Authentication:** Multi-factor authentication (smartcard, PIN, biometrics), Digital Certificate, Private Key, and HSM

- **Authorization:** Credential Issuance (smartcard), Challenge and Response, Public/Private Key pair, and Digital Certificate

- **Non-repudiation:** Multi-factor authentication, Digital Certificate, and Private Key

- **Data integrity:** Hashing, Symmetric ciphers, and Secret Symmetric Key.

- **Signature:** Hashing, Secret Symmetric Key, Digital Certificate, and Private Key

All these additional capabilities come at a cost. If all that is required is authentication for log-on to a computer, server, cloud, application, or Website, you are overpaying for the unused additional functionality, making PKI a very costly solution.

Now, let's look at a cost-efficient infrastructure that offers all the same five elements, but within a confined network.

Symmetric Key Infrastructure (SKI)

Symmetric Key Infrastructure (SKI) is deployed when a limited number of users require authentication into a limited number of managed networks such as Mobile Ad Hoc Wireless Networks (MANET) and peer-to-peer networks. For example doctors, nurses and some staff personnel within a single hospital need patient medical record access and the ability to sign prescriptions or issue medical orders. Because access is within a confined network with a limited number of individuals, and IT has control over who has access, SKI may be the appropriate solution.

SKI has been used for years by financial institutions for secure network-to-network, Point-of-Sale (POS) device to network, and ATM-to-network communications. SKI's use for individual-to-network is relatively new, thanks to the adoption and deployment of smartcards. SKI utilizes multi-factor authentication, symmetric ciphers, hash functions, and HSM. The security of an SKI system relies on keeping the Secret Key secure, not unlike the way PKI keeps the Private Key secure. You will notice that SKI does not require a digital certificate or asymmetric cipher. This keeps the overhead costs down. Here is how SKI accomplishes the five elements:

- **Authentication:** Multi-factor authentication(smartcard, PIN, biometrics), shared Secret Key, and HSM

- **Authorization:** Credential Issuance (smartcard), Challenge and Response, and Secret Key

- **Non-repudiation:** Multi-factor authentication, Secret Key

- **Data integrity:** Hashing, Symmetric Cipher, and Secret Key

- **Signature:** Hashing, and Secret Key

Symmetric ciphers are fast and easy to deploy. The most common way SKI protects the Secret Key is the combination of a user-carried smartcard and a network-installed Secure Access Module (SAM), which is basically a smartcard connected to a server. Multiple Secret Keys can be stored on a single smartcard. Those Keys can also be generated within the organization, so no third-party issuing services are required. What also increases the security of an SKI is that the Secret Key is relatively easy to change, unlike Public/Private Keys.

Key management is probably the greatest concern. If the Secret Key is compromised, then a new Key must be implemented. Because SKI is more than just an authentication protocol, changing a Key can have ripple effects with non-repudiation, data-integrity, and signature. Also, a larger number of nodes connected to the network makes Key distribution and management more of a challenge.

Because SKI manages access only within a closed network, it requires additional functionality, like Single Sign-On, to access other servers, applications, Websites, and clouds. Unfortunately, Single Sign-On occurs behind a network's firewall, which could be a problem for trusted authentication.

Single Sign-On (SSO)

When an employee logs into a company's network/server, she is instantly connected to an Active Directory (AD) database by means of an application protocol called LDAP (Lightweight Directory Access Protocol). Active Directory by Microsoft allows IT to set up and manage an employee's authentication, policies/privileges, directories access, and other Windows services.

SSO uses a single authentication procedure (i.e. User Name and Password) to authenticate a user into Active Directory. Once approved, the employee is then allowed access to other servers, networks, applications, and Websites without the employee having to re-enter any additional User Names or Passwords. Password entry fatigue is resolved. Because IT has full control over Active Directory, they can change all other account passwords daily without any employee knowledge or involvement. This makes SSO a low-level business password manager.

To improve the security of SSO, multi-factor authentication is being incorporated. Companies are adding credentials like ID badges, smartcards, smartphones, and tokens for the possession component of authentication. The knowledge component can be Public Key Infrastructure, One Time Passwords, Symmetric Key Infrastructure, or Password Authentication Infrastructure. All these knowledge-based systems are only as strong as the security that protects their secret. Choosing which option to use is based on your budget, permissions, requirements, number of people, needs, available technologies deployed, and data valuation, to list a few factors.

> **Advantages** - SSO helps get the user out of the role of network security administrator. It adds convenience so that employees do not have to remember, type, generate, or manage any other passwords, except the one that logs them into their computer.

LDAPs and AD are already a part of most server networks, so no additional software needs to be purchased. IT only has to know how to properly configure AD, so there may be minimal training required.

Disadvantages - Single Sign On only works when the computer is online and connected to the server inside the firewall. When authentication takes place inside the firewall, one of your key defenses is removed from the chain of trust, making your effort and expense too late to be secure. The first line of defense should deploy multi-factor authentication before the operating system fully boots up. Once trust is established from user-to-computer and from computer-to-server, then the chain of trust is established.

Active Directory gives a user access to the company's network based on the level of authorization given to them by the IT administrator. Sadly, due to poor configuration or trying to make the computer easier for the employee to use, IT may give everyone administrative rights. This is exactly what a hacker loves because now they can start manipulating other settings and privileges to give themselves full administrative rights while kicking out the company's IT managers. The only way to recover from this type of a breach is to disconnect the server, scrub out all data, and reload everything. It may also require a full scrubbing and reloading of the operating systems, applications, files, etc., of every employee's computer. Depending on the size and severity of the breach, these repairs can take days to weeks or even longer.

SSO can have security flaws if not implemented correctly. IT needs to protect the data using strong verification, anti-virus, encryption, data salting, malware blockers, etc. In recent years, there have been a number of high profile cases where companies, hospitals, government agencies, and others had their databases hacked and user passwords exposed. These attacks demonstrate two vulnerabilities:

1. the lack of properly protecting data; and

2. the high costs of a breach.

SSO does not work with offline computers unless there is some synchronization method to ensure that both databases have the same information. These offline databases also have to use encryption to keep the passwords files safe.

One way to try to make log-on into SSO accounts easier is to leverage off another Website's log-on credentials. The most common one is using a person's

Facebook log-on information. The obvious risk here is that if their Facebook account is ever broken, then everything you thought was protected by your SSO is also now in jeopardy. Since I have already shown what a poor job people do in generating and managing passwords, why would you want to keep your company's information secure by means of Facebook?

One Time Passwords (OTP)

OTPs use either a small, battery-powered device called a dongle with an LCD display, or your smartphone, to show a unique and seemingly random passcode of letters and/or numbers for a short amount of time before a new set of characters are displayed. The user, who is requesting network access from his/her computer, will see a passcode window pop-up on their monitor requesting an account name and the current passcode. If the number they type matches what the server calculated, then access is granted. If not, access is denied. After about 60 seconds, a new number is displayed.

The passcode-generating algorithm is not truly random because it requires a shared secret "seed" to synchronize calculations on both the server and dongle. The passcode number is synchronized to a specific server. Because multiple independent servers cannot be synchronized, no two servers can share the same dongle.

Advantage - The OTP is secure against a brute-force attack. With SSO, employee account log-on is convenient.

Disadvantages - First, dongles are one more thing for employees to carry, forget, or lose. They are also another piece of equipment that IT has to purchase, inventory, and manage. A thief only has to steal a dongle from a known user, go to the network, type in the account name (which is usually a publicly known email address) and then the number displayed. IT cannot block access because a legitimate passcode was entered.

One way the industry tries to eliminate the ability for a hacker to use their computer to log in is by checking the IP address of the specific computer requesting access. Only pre-approved IP address are allowed access, and any new IP requires IT's authorization and approval first. While this does add an additional layer of security, it also adds some inconvenience to employees who have access to multiple computers. Now every computer's IP will have to be added to virtually to every employee's account.

To get around the pre-approved IP list, a hacker can program their computer with any one of the approved IPs in the list. Gathering IP addresses is not that difficult. There are Websites that can help collect that information, and social engineering is another means to get the information. As more specific information becomes generalized and disseminated, it increases the probability of an attack.

Another disadvantage with OTPs is that every server will require its own dongle. Multiple independent servers cannot be synchronized with each other. For example, if you need to access servers belonging to your bank, your company, your vendors, and various shopping sites, you will need a separate dongle for each one. To determine how many unique dongles you will need, count how many different passwords you have.

One way to simplify the use and limit the number of dongles is for the OTP to access an LDAP or a cloud-based password data file and utilize a password manager application. Once the passcode is authenticated, the password manager is controlled through Single Sign-On (SSO). The SSO feature works well here, but you still have to weigh the advantages and disadvantages of SSO, as discussed earlier.

Since the OTP passcode is generated from a specific algorithm, can you really trust that no one else can intercept the code or have a cloned device that sees the same passcode as you do? Again, no network security can block attacks where a legitimate passcode is entered.

⚞ SOMETHING TO THINK ABOUT

In 2011, RSA Security had to replace every one of their 40 million OTP SecurID dongles in use after a successful hack of their algorithm and seed. It was only after the defense contractor Lockheed Martin discovered their security breach and was able to trace it back to RSA Security, did RSA respond.

The sequence of passcodes that a token generates is determined by a secret algorithm and a seed value. Each token has a different seed. Because hackers were able to discover both the algorithm and seed, every dongle became worthless: the chain of trust was broken. With the information the hackers collected, the calculated passcodes can be calculated by any unauthorized computer or server. Reuters even reported that duplicate SecurID tokens were used to attack Lockheed Martin. A statement from an unnamed RSA spokesperson said that was "merely speculation," but gave no additional information.

RSA Security Chairman Art Coviello said that the reason RSA had not disclosed the full extent of the vulnerability earlier was because doing so would have revealed to the hackers how to perform further attacks. However, the Lockheed Martin attack only proved that the hackers knew what they had accomplished, which in turn made other companies unknowingly vulnerable to similar attacks. Customers like Bank of America, Northrop Grumman and L-3 Communications are all rumored to have faced similar attacks. There were also claims that Northrop suspended all remote access to its network for a period of time.

The US Cyber Commander General Keith Alexander in a Congressional hearing on March 27, 2012 pointed to the 2011 RSA Security attack as an example of "Chinese cyber espionage."

Second, many OTP solutions don't actually authenticate the dongle to the computer system. The computer never actually verifies the Have authentication, only the Know. When an employee types in their OTP passcode plus a password, the gatekeeper verifies two Knows. This is called Double-Single-Factor Authentication.

Many of the dongle-based systems are sealed, so batteries cannot be recharged or replaced. Once the battery dies, the only recourse is to purchase another dongle. In addition, IT then has to manage secure, environmental disposal, too.

OTPs do not authenticate the user when a computer first starts up, before the operating system is fully loaded. OTPs require a communications connection between a computer and a server. To reach the server, the user has to get past the firewall. As I've pointed out many times, if you wait to authenticate a visitor until they are past your firewall, you may have just let the hacker in.

Smartphones are now being used to replace the dongle with applications like PhoneFactor® (purchased by Microsoft in 2012) and Google's Authenticator. But how secure are those programs? Employees can easily pick up a virus on their smartphone that can then be used to monitor other activities.

⊞ SOMETHING TO THINK ABOUT

On the Web, there are many articles about viruses running on Google Android phones, iPhones, and every other smartphone. They are picked up by users going to infected Websites, loading infected applications, or even connecting to an infected server. Phones are commonly used to propagate viruses into other networks.

Google reportedly has implemented seven layers of defenses to protect against malware. Their first defense is "Unknown Source" protection. If a Website is accessed and Google is unfamiliar with it, it will block the connections. The problem is that most people turn this feature off because it is inconvenient to get these constant warnings while surfing the Web. Yet another example of convenience trumping security.

Android is not the only vulnerable company. In a Symantec report published in April, 2015, *Internet Security Threat Report*, Volume 20 has classified over 1 million apps as being malware, and 2.3 million a being grayware (technically not malware, but undesirable). Eighty-four percent of the malware targets Apple's iOS, eleven percent Android, four percent BlackBerry, and one percent Nokia/Windows.

Given these statistics, do you really want employee-managed phones logging in to your company's computer networks? Remember, convenience without security is neither secure nor convenient.

Finally, smartphones have a battery life measured in hours or days, where a dongle's battery life is measured in years. If an employee forgets to charge his phone, he would be unable to access the computer network.

Password Authentication Infrastructure

A Password Authentication Infrastructures (PAI) is deployed when an unlimited number of known users requires authentication into an unlimited number of managed networks. PAI combines a password manager with additional security elements designed to keep passwords protected in the same way that cipher keys are protected. Some of these security elements include smartcards, symmetric ciphers, hash functions, secure messages, Key exchanges, and additional functions to make passwords virtually unbreakable.

PAI starts when the computer is first turned on, before the computer operating system fully boots up. With PAI, the user is authenticated at the computer level, outside the company's firewall and the network. Here is how PAI accomplishes Authentication, Authorization, and Non-Repudiation:

- **Authentication:** Multi-factor authentication (smartcard, PIN, biometrics), IT Generated Passwords

- **Authorization:** Credential Issuance (smartcard), Hash, symmetric encryption of data file, Challenge and Response, and IT Generated Passwords

- **Non-repudiation:** Credential Issuance (smartcard), Salted Hash, and IT Generated Passwords

Password authentication systems already exist in virtually every operating system, server, cloud, and application, which makes interfacing a PAI fast and easy. Passwords are used to access LDAP/Active Directory architectures, so a PAI strengthens Single Sign-On log-on security. Because the user does not know or type a password, IT can make them very long and complex, as well as change them frequently.

With a Password Authentication Infrastructure, IT does not have to worry about asymmetric keys, expensive specialized smartcard chips, certificates authorities, registration authorities, revocations lists, or any other outside services that are cumbersome to manage. Everything is contained within the company or agency's network to keep implementation affordable and manageable for IT administrators, and more importantly, convenient and easy for the end-user.

Choosing The Solution That's Right for You

There is no single infrastructure that is right for every company. Choosing the right solution depends on factors like size, type of business, data sensitivity, online activities, and more. The most important takeaway for IT administrators and CISOs is that the different authentication solutions are not mutually exclusive. In fact, they can all be deployed in a tiered approach to best match your employee's security level, needs, and requirements. By layering security, the IT administrator has lower costs of ownership, faster implementation times, and more control over data access security.

In general, most small- and medium-size businesses (SMB) don't need PKI. They don't have the budget, IT personnel, or support to effectively implement and manage PKI. The cybersecurity investment is better spent on authentication, segmenting data based on classification, data file encryption, firewalls, and monitoring. Because of the lower implementation costs of both SKI and PAI, a more appropriate (and customizable) solution can be deployed using the following guidelines for SMBs specifically:

- **Upper management:** SKI and PAI

- **Middle management:** SKI and PAI

- **General employees:** PAI, or SKI/PAI

Large corporations and government agencies will require more PKI capabilities, depending on the security levels of employees and the handling of classified documents and emails. PKI is correct for upper management because it has both legal and fiduciary responsibilities, plus they need access to applications, accounts, internal servers, clouds, and more. These same high-level users also have to deal with password accounts, which means they too would benefit from a Password Authentication Infrastructure. Here are my recommendations for larger entities:

- **Upper Management:** PKI, SKI and PAI

- **Middle management:** SKI and PAI

- **General employees:** PAI, or SKI/PAI

Mid-level managers usually have some fiduciary responsibility, but no legal authority to represent the organization. They typically sign internal documents and need to ensure documentation integrity. Their communications will normally stay within the confines of the internal network, as well as needing access to internal applications. That is why a SKI and PAI combination is appropriate for this group.

Finally, most other employees only require PAI. They have no fiduciary or legal authority. They just need secure authenticated access to computers, data, applications, Websites, and clouds. PAI covers all they need.

PAI works with most existing ID badges, eliminating rebadging costs. Since most log-ons require only a user name and password, no complex integration is required. But best of all, IT now centrally manages all passwords and the employee is no longer the weak link in the cybersecurity chain.

When CISO and IT managers start thinking about layering different technologies, it is vitally important to choose a service provider and vendors who understand all the different authentication infrastructure options. Look for someone who has the knowledge and experience to help you with each of the following points:

- Identifying card technologies that have the growth capabilities you will require for the future

- Making sure all the components you choose are compatible with each other

- Creating a system where <u>every</u> employee has the flexibility to go to any computer and log in

Start thinking of the ID badge as more than just a device that makes a door go beep. The employee ID badge has become a secure, multi-function, multi-application business tool that can increase security, lower your cost of system ownership and revolutionize password management and convenience.

In addition to the above scenarios, there are very small businesses that are required by law to follow strict regulations governing the handling of their data. These include professional offices such as doctors, dentists, attorneys, insurance agents, and a host of others. Even though they may have only one to ten employees, it is mandatory that they do a better job of securing their clients' private information. Having at least a strong PAI is imperative for these businesses because not having one puts them at risk for being shut down by the government, massive fines and penalties that could potentially bankrupt them, and even imprisonment.

CHAPTER 9

RETURN ON YOUR INVESTMENT

"Every time we make an investment decision at FedEx, we ask ourselves: 'What is the return on this investment?'"

~ Frederick W. Smith, President and CEO, FedEx

The two main concerns when implementing cybersecurity are: Technology and Finance. Up to this point, I have concentrated on the technology side, with the intent that the CEO/CFO have a greater understanding of their CISO's world. Now it's time for the CISO and IT administrators to understand how to communicate with the business side.

Talk Business

One of the key benchmarks for any CEO/CFO is Return on Investment (ROI). All expenditures must be justified, and for public companies, it's an important scorecard for shareholders. ROI plays an important role in accounting's Profit and Loss Statement (P&L), Balance Sheet, and Cash Flow Statement.

Ignoring ROI can cause a range of problems. When IT administrators demand the highest level, most expensive, and cumbersome PKI system without a well-informed justification, the company could pay an enormous price (in both time and money) for a system where only a small portion of its capabilities gets utilized. Proposing a solution that's simply too expensive can drive management to ignore or delay IT's request, leaving the company vulnerable. When CEOs make security investment choices on price alone, they could choose a system that does not match their computer security needs, creating a whole new set of problems.

The best strategy is to perform a complete threat assessment of your organization and its infrastructure and then make your business case for the appropriate cybersecurity systems at every level. This chapter will show you how.

⬚ SOMETHING TO THINK ABOUT

You may be familiar with the *Rich Dad, Poor Dad* books by Robert Kiyosaki, where Mr. Kiyosaki describes how his two dads, from different economic backgrounds, perceived and managed wealth in very different ways. While the basic story of having two dads is fictional, I actually had the pleasure of working with the man who was the inspiration behind the "Rich Dad" character, Keith Cunningham.

Keith likes to explain that there are two types of purchases a company can make: Assets and Liabilities. Assets are designed to bring in money. If the thing you buy does not actually bring in money, then it is a liability. While liabilities have their place, too many of them will cause your business to go bankrupt. Cybersecurity, to the business executive, is often considered a liability. The goal of the CISO is to demonstrate to the CEO that security can also be an asset.

Every year, IT managers request increased budgets to safeguard their company's network from the latest threats. All too often, the CEO/CFO believe they have already invested enough and refuse to allocate additional funds. No matter how urgent the need for additional cybersecurity, if the business side cannot justify the funding, IT's request will not get approved.

Many IT managers do not understand business and many CFOs do not understand the complexity of computer networks. It's as if IT is from Mercury and CFOs are from Pluto. So instead of justifying your budget with FUD (fear, uncertainty, and doubt) like telling horror stories about how hackers broke into another company's network, IT administrators need to take a page from the finance geek's playbook and talk about profit and loss and how security affects the company's bottom line. It's really not that difficult. And you can do it honestly by using real numbers and not wild speculations. I have a tool for that which I'll share with you shortly.

Here's the final test. Once you determine your ROI numbers, cut the loss in half to cover any incorrect assumptions. If the cost of a breach is still painful, then you know your proposal will be considered.

⚏ SOMETHING TO THINK ABOUT

Years ago, I worked with a company's IT department that needed to invest in more security. Their IT manager grumbled that their CEO would not justify any more spending on security because his main focus was increasing sales. I said, "Great, let's talk to him. Will you ask him to attend our meeting?"

At our meeting, the CEO's main argument was that he needed more customers, and more network security was not going to accomplish that goal.

My approach was simple. If his company experienced a data breach, then thirty percent of his existing customers would immediately move over to his competitors. I suggested that by marketing the idea that his company puts customer security at the forefront, he can attract new customers. And when his competitors have a breach, their customers are likely to move over to him.

After training his sales team to understand and discuss the benefits of their company's new increased security policies, I followed up six months later. I was told that the company experienced a 40% increase in new customers and a 27% improvement in existing customer retention. While every business is different, there are ways for cybersecurity to improve a business's P&L.

Breaking Down the Costs of a Breach

Business owners understand the importance of physical security. An intruder affects tangible assets. The security officer's responsibility is to protect the company, force a thief to either look elsewhere, or identify and contain him for the authorities.

These are some of the typical physical security investments:

- Physical access control systems
- Door locks
- Employee ID badges
- Paper shredders
- Locking file cabinets
- Alarm system
- CCTV
- Fences
- Gates
- Guards
- Patrol service
- Insurance
- And the list goes on

To create the same level of understanding about cybersecurity, IT must first start linking employees' hours of computer usage to salary. If IT has to shut down the network to fix a breach, then employees are idle while still receiving their salary. A single breach may take hours or even days to fix. Second, coordinate with the sales department about their forecasted revenue for a new product. Turn that valuation into lost revenue forecasts if a competitor got access to the company's R&D data. Finally, what would happen to the company's reputation with their customers if internal emails were made public? Not sure? Just ask Sony. For the CEO and CFO, it's not about the nature of the threat, but rather the business ramifications.

According to the National Cyber Security Alliance (https://www.staysafeonline.org/), in 2014, sixty percent of SMBs were out of business within six months after experiencing a data breach. Most of these companies did not have the capital, technical talent on staff, or any idea how to properly respond to their data breach. What makes this statistic even more alarming is that seventy-one percent of all data breaches target small businesses, making data breaches the new "company killer."

To explain the true cost of a data breach, let's divide the losses into six operational categories. No one category is more important than any other. Rather, they are all interdependent and integrated with each other.

The six categories are:

- Reputation
- Financial
- Legal/Regulatory
- Operational
- Technology
- Business

Direct costs are much easier for corporate executives to understand, but those account for only thirty-three percent of the losses. Indirect costs contribute up to sixty-seven percent of the costs of a data breach. This is where IT can shine by helping upper management understand the extent and ramifications of these indirect costs.

Where Did All the Money Go

In 2013, the average cost to a United States business after a data breach was approximately $5.4 million per incident ($188 per record). In 2014, the average jumped to $5.85 million ($201 per record) (Ponemon: "2014 Cost of Data Breach Study: Global Analysis"). The FBI has claimed 2015 as the year of the cyber hack, which is why I anticipate the 2015 costs to exceed $6 million per incident.

Throwing out high numbers like these does little to no good convincing any CEO to buy more security. Some will argue that their business is not large enough for these costs to apply to them. These costs are only averages, which means some losses were higher and some were lower. To better understand how a data breach affects a company's financial wellbeing, let's drill down into the six operations categories mentioned above.

Keep these questions in mind as you review the list:

- How much was already spent in time and money (including employee salaries) to acquire your current customers, vendors, and suppliers?

- How much will it cost to attract back a lost customer, vendor, or supplier?

- How much will it cost to get new customers with bad news posted on the Internet?

- Where will the money to pay for issues associated with a data breach come from?

- What planned activities to gain new customers will you have to postpone? And what revenues were those activities expected to bring in?

A complete graph of all the categories and their associated expenses can be found on our Website at https://www.access-smart.com/wp-content/uploads/2015/03/ROI-Cost-Chart.jpg.

Reputation:

Your business reputation is your number one asset. It determines your trustworthiness, whether customers will want your goods or services, and the long-term likelihood of both customers and vendors staying with you. Reputation costs can be broken down into:

- Loss of vendors and suppliers
- Loss of customers
- Loss of strategic partners
- Loss of staff
- Loss of new customers

Financial:

Your finances will be hit with new costs and expenditures that you probably did not budget for. Long-term goodwill and special pricing will be affected, especially if vendors drop you and you have to find new ones. Plus, the state and/or federal regulations may require that they monitor your company, imposing new auditing fees and activities. You will have to pay for credit monitoring services for all your customers and employees. That was probably never budgeted. You may need to raise new money, deplete savings, or divert allocated funds to pay for these new activities. If you take out loans, then there are new interest payments, as well.

Here are just a few of the new financial costs:

- Cost of Remediation
- Cost of Communications
- Cost of Insurance
- Cost of New Deductible Rate
- Cost of Changing Vendors
- Cost of Business Distractions
- Firing/Layoff Employee Compensations
- Multi-year Credit Monitoring for all your customers

Legal/Regulatory:

Lawyers are always involved when there is a breach. Think about lawsuits, reviewing press statements, representation to the state and federal courts and agencies. The skills required are probably not those of your general counsel, so specialists will need to be hired. Costs include:

- Federal fines and penalties for compliancy violations
- State fines and penalties
- Cost of Lawsuits
- Loss of Accreditations or Certifications
- Review of correspondence

Operations:

A data breach will also affect the day-to-day operations of your business. Business-as-usual changes, employee responsibilities change, and employees get pulled off projects to help put out fires. Most of these expenses divert funds away from winning new customers, bringing new products to market, or keeping ahead of your competitors. It's all about damage control. Associated costs include:

- Cost of Firing Personnel
- Cost of Layoffs
- Loss of Productivity
- Cost of Recruiting New Hires
- Cost of Processing New Hires
- Cost of Training New Hires
- Annual Audit Costs

Technology:

If there is a breach, computers, networks and applications will need to be upgraded, replaced, or supplemented, requiring more off-budget money being spent. Those expenses include:

- Costs to Upgrade Old Equipment
- Cost to Purchase and Install New Equipment
- Training Costs on New Equipment
- Hiring Web Monitoring Services

Business:

This is the catchall category. A data breach will not only affect your customers, but also any current or future investors, and the caliber of any new hires. It doesn't matter if your company is publicly or privately held; these costs can put the final nail into your bankruptcy coffin with:

- Loss of Existing Marketing and Advertisement Investments
- Loss of Investors
- Bad Press
- Drop in Stock Prices
- Drop in Company Valuation
- Loss of Integrity

A major roadblock between upper management and IT has been the lack of ROI justification to management for additional IT security spending. Security is similar to insurance. It might be hard to justify the month after month expenses, until you need it.

The uniqueness of every industry and organization makes it difficult to create a one size fits all ROI calculator. Here is how Ponemon's *2014 Cost of Data Breach Study: Global Analysis* report breaks down the $5.85M cost per incident:

- $417,700 is the average detection and escalation cost in the US

- $509,237 is the average notification cost in the US

- $1,599,996 is the average post-data breach cost in the US

- $3,324,959 is the average lost business cost in the US

Cybersecurity is not just about technology, hackers, and encryption. As an engineer in the defense industry, I designed everything from both a strategic and a tactical perspective. In the world of cybersecurity, financial considerations are the strategic part and technology is the tactical part. One without the other will result in either overpaying for security that may not protect your network's vulnerabilities, or underfunding IT to the point where your company is vulnerable.

Business managers must begin to understand cybersecurity from a working perspective and IT managers need to understand basic financial principles. The integrated management of these two groups will go a long way toward eliminating or at least containing what a hacker can do to you.

CHAPTER 10

IMPLEMENTING A MULTI-FACTOR PASSWORD AUTHENTICATION INFRASTRUCTURE

"If you don't know where you are going, you might wind up someplace else."

~ Yogi Berra, baseball icon

PAI combines the strengths of a password manager, symmetric encryption, hashing, Diffie-Hellman, and smartcards, making it both secure and cost-effective. PAI is designed to leverage off many of your existing computer and network components, including the operating system, browsers, applications, and most importantly, your existing employee ID card. Typically, there is no new server hardware to purchase, no upgrading applications, and no intensive IT retraining. These benefits alone lower the cost-of-ownership, increase the ease of implementation, and improve the employee's ease-of-use. PAI is a simple drop-in and play installation that typically takes less than two hours to fully install and start implementing.

Before installing a PAI system, there are five components IT must understand and define. They are:

- Cards – typically employee ID badges and determined by desired applications

- Card Readers – the interface between the card and the computer

- Password Manager software – the brains behind removing the weakest link

- Password Administrator software – the IT control center

- Industry Standards and Specifications – ensures compliance to government regulations

Start with the Card

I start with cards because many companies already use ID card badges for physical access. Smartcards are the most versatile and diverse of all the cards. There are contact and contactless cards, cards with operating systems and cards without. There are single technology cards and hybrid cards. While all this may sound confusing, it really isn't.

Whenever I consult with a new client, I usually start by asking two questions: "What do you currently do with your existing cards, and what would you like to do with those cards in the future?" Their answers begin defining a card's specifications because application determines technology, not the other way around. Here are just some of the more common uses for cards and the typical smartcard technologies deployed:

- Physical Access - contactless

- Cyber Access - contact or contactless

- ePayments - contact or contactless

- Parking - contactless

- Membership and loyalty - contact or contactless

- Secure document printing - contactless

- Time and Attendance - contactless

- Vehicle ignition systems - contactless

- Transit - contactless

After defining the desired applications, I ask more questions to understand a few other factors like usage environment, existing infrastructure, and budgets. All of these influence card choice. Once all the upfront requirements are known, it's time to start choosing the card technology.

Smartcard Technologies

Smartcards come in two different forms: contact and contactless. Contact smartcards require the user to physically insert the card into a reader. Contact cards have more memory storage than contactless, can process advanced calculations faster, and are better when dealing with authentication issues like Challenge and Response. Contact cards are not appropriate in high traffic applications where a high volume of card insertions and removals are required. They are also not great for environments where debris, rain, or corrosive elements could deteriorate the reader. If you have one of the new credit cards with a little gold chip on it, then you have a contact smartcard in your wallet.

Contactless smartcards, on the other hand, require no physical connection to a reader. They utilize radio frequency (RF) fields, which work well in harsher environments and high traffic areas. They are used primarily for small data transfers that need to be done quickly. Contactless cards have limited memory capabilities, do not do extensive calculations well, and may not be appropriate for some advanced security applications like PKI. If you have waved your ID badge, or seen an employee wave his, over a door reader that unlocks the door, that's contactless technology at work.

Contact smartcards are divided into three classifications: cards with secure memory chips (memories), microcontroller chips (micros), and crypto-controller chips (cryptos). Memories are the simplest and can be thought of as a floppy disk or thumb drive on a card. They have very limited processing capabilities. Micros are little minicomputers that have their own operating system, RAM, ROM, and data communication protocols. I equate micros to having a small computer in your wallet. Cryptos are similar to microcontrollers, but with the addition of specialized circuits to calculate advanced cryptographic algorithms typically found in PKI.

These three kinds of contact smartcards get sub-divided based on memory size and operating systems. When it comes to cost, the memory chips are the cheapest and the cryptos are the most expensive. Within each family, the amount of memory available with determine price. More memory equals higher prices. Finally, for both the micros and cryptos, the chip's operating system also affects price. Some operating systems are open and some are proprietary. All things considered, a smartcard can range in cost from less than a dollar each for memories in high volumes, up to about thirty dollars each for cryptos.

If for no other reason than cost, you need to define your application ahead of time. You don't want to buy an expensive chip when you only need ten percent of its full capabilities. You will also want to avoid investing in cards that cannot grow with your needs. There are many consultants in the market who can help you with your choice. I list a few on my Website that I personally know and trust.

For contactless technology, the main considerations are: frequency, read range, memory, and read/write capabilities. Contactless cards use two main frequencies: 125kHz, and 13.56MHz. Physical access was built on the 125kHz proximity (Prox) technology. It is a read-only technology with a short read range of 10cm. By today's security standards, it is considered weak. Prox has no memory size options. Because the marketplace is requiring higher security, read/write, and multi-application capabilities, Prox is being phased out and replaced by the newer 13.56MHz higher frequency cards.

The higher frequency cards are classified by two different industry specifications: ISO/IEC 14443 and ISO/IEC 15693. Both offer read/write capabilities, security features, and various memory sizes. (The memory available on contactless chips is not as large as those on contact chips.) The main difference between these two specs is read range. 14443 has a read distance less than 10cm. 15693 has read distance less than 100cm. Some vendor products are designed to these open standards while others have added protocols that make them proprietary to a specific manufacturer. Be sure to do your research before getting locked into a proprietary system that will make you a slave to one vendor and become too expensive to ever migrate away from.

Finally, the card industry understands that no one solution works for every customer. That's why you can also purchase hybrid cards that contain various mixtures of different technologies within one card. It is not unusual to combine a contact and contactless card. I have also run across customers who need a contact chip, two contactless technologies (125kHz and 13.56MHz), and a magnetic stripe all on the same card. Again, application, environment, existing infrastructure, and budget will determine the most appropriate card for you.

Why Smartcards for Multi-Factor Authentication?

Today's cybersecurity requires multi-factor authentication. Having a card alone is not secure enough without also verifying that the person in possession of the card is authorized to have the card. With a smartcard, the employee must also know a secret (like a PIN), present their fingerprint for comparison against data stored within the card, or maybe both. These functions often require read/write and processing capabilities, something the older 125 kHz Prox cards cannot do. In these situations, all the calculations have to be done outside the card and inside the reader or computer. Because I strongly believe that a person's identifiers should remain in their possession, I recommend smartcards for cyber access.

How Layers of Authentication Build Trust

Once multi-factor authentication has been accomplished between the user and the card, the next step is a handshake between the card and the computer. Smartcards easily handle this next layer of multi-factor authentication. The computer detects the presence of the card (Something the computer Has). The card has unique identifiers (Something the card Is) that the computer will only accept when verified. Finally, the smartcard contains passwords, Keys, hash seeds and a number of other secrets (Something the card Knows) which the user does not know.

So, what just happened? First, the person verifies himself to the card. Then, the computer looks at the card to identify Something that the card Is. The computer uses data the card Knows to authorize access from the card to the computer. Then, from computer to card.

The final step is to perform mutual Challenge-Response calculations from card-to-server and server-to-card. The server sends a piece of information to calculate a value. That value is sent back to the server for comparison. If they match, then the server knows the card is authorized. This process is then reversed where the card sends a piece of information. If the server calculates the same value, then the card knows the server is legit.

Putting all these processes together creates three independent layers of multi-factor authentication: User-to-Card, Card-to-Computer, and Card-to-Server.

Later, when you add a password manager, you will also know that the person logging into applications is the person they say they are because the password manager knows and enters the correct (complex) passwords, independent of the end-user. The password manager fixes the weakest link in your chain of trust: the employee or end-user.

Putting it all together

PKI and SKI require smartcard technologies to safeguard their Keys because of their many advanced security features. If smartcards are safe enough to protect cypher keys, then they surely can protect passwords.

The takeaways regarding smartcards are simple. Start by first assessing your specific use and application. One smartcard technology is not necessarily better than another. The cards you choose will be based on your requirements. Next, build on as much of your existing infrastructure as possible. And last, consider hybrid cards that can be customized with a mix of all the different applications you require.

Once the card specs have been determined, how it will communicate with the computer needs to be determined. That is where readers come in.

Reader Technologies

Choosing the correct reader is straightforward. The reader is determined by the card technology and the computer connection. Is the card using a contact chip, contactless technology, or something else? Is the computer connection via a USB port, Bluetooth, PCMCIA, ExpressCard, or something else?

Contact smartcard readers come in a wide variety of styles and functionalities. There are stand-alone readers, readers built into keyboards, lightweight travel readers, heavy-base desktop readers for easy one-handed insertion and removal, and readers that fit inside the computer. The reader supplies power, commands, timing, and data transfer to the card through metal contacts. Choose the reader that best suits the environment where it will be used.

⊞ SOMETHING TO THINK ABOUT

Not too long ago, I was contacted by a sewage and waste disposal company to secure their network logins. As part of the government's push to secure our nation's infrastructure, their concern was preventing a hacker from getting into their network and discharging sewage into the clean reclaimed water. What seemed like an easy fit for contact cards had an environmental condition that could easily have been overlooked.

The decomposition of waste makes the surrounding air acidic. That acid is known to corrode metal quickly. Contact readers would have a much shorter lifespan and the company would have to constantly replace them. The solution was hermetically sealed, contactless cards and readers.

Contactless smartcard readers have a wide variety of styles. The part you have to watch here is the card's operating frequency. Prox 125kHz cards don't work with 13.56MHz readers, and vice versa. There are vendors who have developed multi-frequency readers, but they are more expensive than single frequency ones. Knowing what card will be used for each application can save your budget. These radio frequency (RF) readers broadcast a specific frequency. The card has an antenna coil and tiny silicon chip embedded between the layers of plastic that is tuned to that frequency. When the card comes within range of the RF field, the reader is able to supply power to the card's chip, establish a communication connection, and transfer data. In some ways, it works like a small radio station and car radio.

Most computers have USB ports, making a USB connector the interface you will likely use from reader-to-computer. Older laptops used PCMCIA and ExpressCard connectors. Many of today's new tablets, smartphones, and the barrage of Internet of Things (IoT) are using Bluetooth, WiFi, mini-USB, and micro-USB. The larger reader manufacturers have solutions for most, if not all of these interfaces.

Putting it all together

There are many reader manufacturers in the industry, and as smartcards become more mainstream, the cost of readers is coming down. Once you know your card types, frequency and computer connection types, here are some additional considerations:

- PC/SC compliant readers. This industry standard allows for seamless integration to a computer's operating system. Otherwise, custom drivers have to be used.

- Operational use. Consider how much desktop space the reader takes up, is it going to be placed in a briefcase, and how easy is it for the employee to present his card.

- Purchase cards and readers from the same supplier. Like computers, smartcards and readers have slight variations. Think of it like an Apple

Mac and a Windows PC. Similar hardware functionality may not be physically interchangeable.

Cards and readers are used only to authenticate and authorize the user. Once that is done, something else is required for the remaining processes of cybersecurity. It's time to discuss the brains behind Password Authentication Infrastructure—The Password Manager.

Password Manager Software

A password manager is one of the simplest ways to secure passwords. Unfortunately, the majority of these products are <u>not</u> designed for professional, enterprise, or government use. Many password managers are consumer grade, and are nothing more than glorified spreadsheets from which a user copies and pastes their log-on information into the appropriate field. A few are highly intelligent and can recognize when a log-on field appears and know how and when to auto-form fill. Very few password managers bother to check the address or path of the application to verify that it is legitimate before releasing data. Finally, even fewer vendors use government approved encryption verified by independent security labs, smartcards, multi-factor authentication, and secure communication protocols to prevent third-party eavesdropping.

A good enterprise password manager must address both sides of the security fence: the end-user "client" side and the IT administration side. The client portion should make log-on convenient, nonintrusive, and secure, in that order. Imagine the delight of an employee being able to simply double-click which server, Website, or application they want to access, and then watch as the program auto-launches the application and auto-fills their user name and password, which they do not even have to know. The employee just sits back and watches it happen.

Filling in passwords is easy, but network security is paramount. IT has to protect employees, and their network, from viruses, malware, spam, phishing, bogus links, social engineering, and all the other attacks discussed in previous chapters. Here are some other considerations when choosing an enterprise level password manager:

- How easy is the installation and use of the application?

- Does it include a token for multi-factor authentication?

- Do you have to carry a second token or will it work with your existing one (like your employee ID badge)?

- Where and how are your passwords stored, and are they stored securely?

- Should you trust a third party's shared server to store your passwords, or should you store your passwords within your own network?

- Is the software customizable to match your specific business environment and policies? Or do you have to adapt your situation to their software policies?

- Does it meet industry-recognized security specification like FIPS?

- If the token is ever lost or stolen, how easy is it for someone to retrieve the data? How easy is it for the user to get a replacement token?

- If you use a device like a smartphone to receive a passphrase, what happens if the user forgets to charge his phone?

Password Administrator Software

If the password manager is the brains, then the password administrator software is the heart of PAI. The administrator software is what IT managers use to set and configure the password manager to have it abide by the company's cybersecurity policies and procedures. The complexity of passwords, the change frequency of passwords, length, and all the other considerations discussed in earlier chapters should all be configurable. Don't allow solutions providers to dictate your company's security policies based on their software's capabilities. You relinquish the ability to address your specific threats and risks that might be unique to your company or industry.

IT centrally managed passwords block the employee from knowing, remembering, or typing any passwords. If the employee does not know any passwords, then social engineering attacks are futile. A robust password administration software should be able to perform, at a minimum, the following functions:

- Confirm authorized links and paths to Websites, servers, and applications

- Centralize management service for issuance, lost, stolen, damaged, or forgotten cards

- Policy implementation service

- Lifecycle management service

- Access reporting service

- Import employee data from other databases to eliminate multiple database entries, mistyped information, and higher overhead costs

- Set the strength, complexity and change frequency of passwords, making employees automatically abide by their security policies.

- Customized password generator

- License transfers to accommodate employee turnover at no additional cost. (Not possible with a digital certificate.)

With today's privacy and data protection laws (HIPAA, HITECH, CJIS, SOX, and many other government regulations) requiring compliance from every business, consumer-grade password managers cannot safeguard your company from a data breach. And if you do experience a breach, government officials may determine you did not follow industry best practice guidelines and slap you with heavy fines and penalties.

Putting it all together

Creating a Password Authentication Infrastructure involves more than just throwing together cards, readers, and password managers and expecting it all to work. PAI requires a level of informed knowledge about how all the many pieces fit together and interoperate.

In addition to sorting out all the components, a PAI must be many things to many people. From the employee's perspective, PAI must be Convenient, Secure, and Affordable, in that order. IT will require Security first, followed by Convenience and Affordability. Finally, the business managers will want Affordability, followed by Convenience and Security. The good news is, it's doable.

Security Specifications and Standards

In addition to state and federal governments passing many new security regulations, large corporations have now begun requiring their suppliers to improve their security in order to do business with them. Industry-recognized specifications and standards help ensure that your PAI solution will withstand any audits or compliance issues, whether they be government or corporate. The following section provides a handy checklist.

Companies offering security products must meet industry security standards. These standards allow for interoperability with other hardware and software and deliver a layer of trust. Look for products that have been tested by trusted security labs and meet government requirement verifications. While some of these security specifications may not be required within your particular industry, and could add additional costs to a solution, they do show that the company is serious about security. Some of the approvals to look for are:

- FIPS 140-2

- FIPS 201

- AES-265 encryption or higher (DES is no longer acceptable)

- SHA-256 encryption

- Windows Server Enhanced Cryptography

- Mutual authentication between client and server applications

- Encryption of client/server application communications

- Hashing of PINs

- Salting of Passwords

- Encryption of login credentials

- Secure Socket Layers (SSL)

- Microsoft SQL Server 2014 certification

- Windows compatibility verification from Microsoft

Many of today's projects and bids call out these and other industry specifications. After the recent Target breach, many large corporations are imposing these security standards on their suppliers if they want to continue being a supplier.

The technology and implementation of PAI is important to IT and somewhat interesting to everyone else. Because cybersecurity has both a technical and business aspect, let's discuss the advantages for the business side.

The ROI of PAI

PAI has many unique ROI savings that both accounting and IT find very attractive. Probably the biggest one is reduced help-desk calls. In a large corporation, IT can spend an average of seven to eight hours a week on issues related to passwords. Thirty to forty percent of that time is spent resetting forgotten passwords. According to *Network World Magazine's January 5, 2015 article by Ann Bednarz "15 Job Titles Getting Big Salary Boosts in 2015," the* salary range for an **information systems security manager is** $122,250-$171,250 per year. So your employee-managed passwords could cost your company roughly $21,394-$34,250 a year from IT alone. This does not include the time employees cannot work on their computers because they are waiting for IT to solve their problem.

Now, let's analyze the cost of implementation. Because a PAI can build on existing infrastructures, there is very little additional hardware or server modification required. Look for a product that is card- and reader-agnostic. If you already have a proximity, RFID, or contact smartcard system deployed, you only need an enterprise password manager that works with your credential. Why should you buy new cards when your existing ones may work just fine? This saves both time and money over rebadging, re-issuing, controller re-programming, and disposal costs. Depending on the size of the company and the extensiveness of the change, rebadging may cost $12,000 to $50,000.

Another cost is employee enrollment. Expecting employees to go to a designated computer, visit IT, or any number of other scenarios that do not allow for self-enrollment can add to deployment costs. The better solution is one that allows for employee self-enrollment from their own computer station. The employee simply turns on their computer, presents their card, and fills out a simple form, at which point a license is linked to the card. This typically takes only a couple of minutes, with little to no employee productivity loss. Once enrollment is verified, IT now has centralized management of that card's policies and account passwords. That simple "qwerty" password is now something resembling "ZdY9Jd+1PuhWnK=c`gmE."

Every company at one time or another will experience employee turnover. Some organizations, like schools, contractors, and stores that hire seasonal workers, can experience very high turnover. If the company has to buy new licenses every time their old users leave and new ones come in, the cost of ownership soon becomes prohibitive. A PAI system needs to take turnover into account. Look for an enterprise password manager with transferable licenses.

Here are a few case studies where customers found value by implementing a PAI solution.

PAI Case Studies

Carlos Rosario International Charter School

The Carlos Rosario International Charter School aims to provide education that prepares the diverse adult immigrant population of Washington, DC to become invested, productive citizens and members of American society. With 1,200 to 1,500 students per year, it is one of the few accredited adult education schools in the country.

Part of the learning curriculum at the school is to get students comfortable with technology by accessing personal computers in any of the six computer labs or thirty classrooms on the premises. Like many environments with multiple users and multiple computers, the students and staff had been logging onto the computers using their own unique user names and passwords. However, this resulted in a considerable amount of wasted time, money, and resources for the IT staff resetting forgotten passwords and unlocking computers that had locked due to the user not logging off properly.

In order to find a method that would make computer access easier for the students, less time-consuming for teachers and the IT department, while still maintaining a secure network, Karen Clay, IT Director for the school, began looking for a user authentication solution that could meet very specific criteria unique to her particular environment.

"Many of our students are new to the country and have not used a computer before," said Clay. "I knew we needed a system in place that would grant students computer access without adding any more responsibility on their shoulders. Not only that, but this system would have to streamline our administrative functions and be cost-effective in terms of reducing the time spent on network access issues."

The system she chose could be integrated into the network's Active Directory so students could initiate secure and easy access to the network using any student computer on the premises. At each station, a small card reader plugs into the USB port of the desktop, and the student simply inserts their card, which grants them access. When the students remove their cards, their account is automatically closed, which prevents unauthorized access to the network and enables the computer to be ready for the next student to log on.

"A major selling point for me on the PAI system was the card itself," said Clay. "The students are already required to carry a student ID card to enter the facility. We print the student photo and identification information on one side, load their computer log-in information on the other, and they have only one card to keep track of. In addition, the system did not involve any back-end installation or existing network modifications that would have been cumbersome for my department to install and maintain. Since I can recycle card licenses, the overall maintenance costs are low, and I like the fact that it's scalable and will grow with our school's needs in the future."

Delaware Doctor Finds Solution to Network Security Concerns

by Neil S. Kalin, MD

I am a practicing ophthalmologist in Delaware, and like many solo docs, I am also the in-house IT manager. The government has encouraged all of us to adopt EMR. About two years ago, I went "all-in" with electronic medical records (EMR) software. One of the scariest things about this process is the penalties levied by the government for a failed security audit or data breach.

I have read stories of medical practices losing a hard drive or laptop and then being fined over $100,000. In addition, many major hospitals with fulltime IT security teams have been fined millions of dollars for a breach. The US government does not treat protecting patient's records lightly. I have been quite pleased with my EMR software; however, the system does not require a "strong" password for access. HIPAA guidelines recommend the standard security components like anti-virus software, firewalls, and strong passwords but they also discussed "multi-factor authentication."

One of my greatest concerns was that when the patient was in the exam room behind a closed door, they could access my PC or network. Having a running desktop PC behind a closed door is sometimes just too tempting for a patient. They want to just check their e-mail or quickly surf the Web. However, they could also check medical files. With HIPAA's requirement of preventing unauthorized access into patient files, I knew I needed a solution that would stand up to an audit. My security auditor recommended that I "lock" Windows whenever I left the room. While this step may be "best practices," I was concerned about how much it would slow me down to enter the password so many times each day.

Enter Password Authentication Infrastructure product Power LogOn® by Access Smart. This ingenious product promised both security and user convenience for logging into computers, applications, and networks without having to remember or type a user name or password. This solution uses smartcard-based, multi-factor authentication. Access Smart also has a money-back guarantee. I took the plunge and purchased their Power LogOn Administrator Starter Kit. I was able to use the smartcards and readers that I had already purchased and only needed the software from them.

Power LogOn has simplified life for me and my staff. Before we leave the exam room, we simply push Window/L and Windows is locked. When the staff or I need to access the computer, we swipe a prox card and automatically are logged into *both* Windows and the EMR. Everyone has a unique card and password and we can track who and when a person has accessed the computer or network.

I searched for other products and Power LogOn is really the only solution that I have found that addresses HIPAA security **and** user's convenience. It was easy to install and the Access Smart team was there to answer any questions that came up. Power LogOn is a reliable, cost-effective solution to enhance network security. I now feel much better knowing that my patients (behind closed doors) are not jeopardizing my practice with a HIPAA violation now that Power LogOn is deployed.

PAI Countermeasures to Password Attacks

In Chapter 6, you learned about the different attacks that are used to break passwords. Here is how PAI addresses those attacks:

- **Password Uniqueness** – A PAI should utilize a random password generator that includes uppercase, lowercase, numbers and special characters. Plus, the quantity of each of type of character can be designated. For example, an IT administrator can set parameters like: the fifteen-character generated password has to have a minimum of 5 uppercase, 3 lowercase, 2 special characters, 2 numbers, and the remaining three characters could be any one of these types randomly picked by the computer.

Unique passwords block:

- **Brute-Force Attack** – Easy implementation of much longer passwords. For example, to match Private Key security, use 32-character passwords.

- **Dictionary Attacks** – Passwords can be generated using any of the 256 ASCII codes. No more spelling of words or personal association to the user.

- **Over-the-Shoulder Surfers** – User does not type any passwords, so there's nothing to see. While they may see the PIN, a surfer must also be in possession of the card. If this is a concern for IT, then a biometric authenticator can also be included.

- **Keyloggers** – User doesn't type passwords, so there is nothing for a keylogger to capture.

- **Password Storage** – passwords should be securely stored in smartcards, or in LDAP where they are encrypted and salted. When a password log-on is requested, only that one password should be decrypted and not the entire file. The entire password file should never be decrypted and cached in RAM. Secure storage addresses the following attacks:

  - **Sticky Note Security** – When employees do not generate or know any passwords, they don't have the need to write anything down.

  - **Storing passwords in the Browser** – Passwords are no longer stored in the browser. They are stored inside a smartcard, HSM or encrypted and salted inside an LDAP.

- **Social Engineering** – If the employee does not know any of their passwords, there is nothing they can tell.

- **Unencrypted Email Intercepts** – Again, since the employee is out of the role of password manager, there are no passwords they can email. Any needs now have to go through IT to approve.

- **Account Redirect Protection** – A PAI needs to check that the server domain, IP Address, URL, or application path is legitimate before releasing any confidential log-on information. Account address checking safeguards against:

  - **Spamming, Phishing, and Pharming** – When the PAI first checks a site's URL address against what it knows, any links or log-on addresses that do not match the PAI will not autofill.

- **Limit Password Lifetime** – IT can change passwords every day if they determine that is required. Frequent password changes are the best defense against a Pass the Hash attack. IT can make changes in the background, and the user never knows any of it.

  - **Rainbow Table Attack** – Most PAIs salt the password Hash using unique information found inside the smartcard. Building a hash table would be useless.

  - **Remote Administrator Tools (RAT), Cross-site scripting (XSS), and Lumping all data together** – These are not really password problems but IT administration issues. Secure passwords, password encrypted files, and salting add layers of complexity.

- **Password Exchange** – Sharing of the password secret is handled the same way Symmetric Keys are exchanged, by using any of the approved Key exchange protocols, like Diffie-Hellman.

Important Considerations

When it comes to security and security products, there are many product choices, pricing models, and services available. One is not necessarily better than another. The question is, which one is right for you? In this section, I am going to cover some of the more common solutions and what you want to consider before purchasing. These are only my opinions and you know what they say about opinions.

Software as a Service (SaaS):

Many security software companies follow the Software as a Service (SaaS) pricing model of monthly or annual subscription fees. It is my opinion that PAI solutions are best when owned and managed within an organization. Should the security vendor go out of business or be acquired, you do not want your log-on services to abruptly stop, leaving your network vulnerable to attacks and your IT administrator scrambling for a replacement service.

Third-Party Storage of Passwords:

To make management of passwords easier and available on mobile devices, one strategy is to have password files stored in a cloud server and hosted by a third party. The conveniences of this model make some sense, but there are also some cautions.

When passwords are stored and managed by a third-party vendor, you could lose all control of password security. You have to rely on both their physical and computer security. Their servers may be located overseas where ownership laws may differ from those in the US. Finally, they may co-locate your password files on shared server hard drives with another company's data, which makes you susceptible to that other company's security practices. An attack that was targeting one of their customers could end up jeopardizing every customer.

Finally, as the number of customers using a cloud password manager increases, so does the number of stored passwords. In other words, a huge repository of passwords attracts hackers like a bee to a flower. On June 15, 2015, LastPass announced that hackers broke into their computer system and got access to their customers' email addresses, password reminders, and encrypted versions of people's master passwords. While LastPass did deploy many security measures and they are now adding HSM devices to protect their encryption keys, it shows that big data attacks can harm many companies and individuals.

The cloud model for mobile devices has merit, but you want a dedicated server, located where your laws apply, and safeguarded by your encryption keys. Security involves not just preventing a hacker from stealing a data file, but also making that data worthless should they get it.

Carrying Multiple Credentials:

Business executives often ask me if employees should carry multiple credentials and dongles: one for photo ID, one for physical access control, and now one for cyber access. My answer is, "No." The more devices a person carries, the more inconvenient it is for the employee, the greater the risk of the credential being lost, stolen, or forgotten, and the more devices IT has to manage and stock.

I once worked on a project where I created a single, multi-technology card that included physical access, logical access, payment, time and attendance, and forklift vehicle ignition. The first four items were standard applications, but we added a function that required a forklift operator to present his card to a reader located on the dash. If the operator was non-union and did not have the proper training, the vehicle would not start. This saved the company on insurance premiums and satisfied the unions.

I have also worked with companies wanting to add secure printing and copying. Have you ever been working on a customer's account that contains sensitive information? When finished, you sent the document to a shared printer, but got distracted and forgot to pick it up until hours later? For some industries, this is a major security violation with severe government penalties and fines. Now with smartcards, printing occurs only when the employee presents her card to the printer's reader. Besides securing the document, the proper department can be billed for the paper and ink costs.

Integration with Third-Party Products:

There are many great third-party software applications on the market. Some are specialized for a particular industry like healthcare's Electronic Medical Records (EMR), real estate's Property Management, and law enforcement's Record Management Systems (RMS). There are also general applications like accounting software, file encryption, and secure email programs. What they all have in common is password authentication. A good PAI system will also offer Application Programming Interface (API) to third-party vendors allowing for an integrated multi-factor authentication solution. When PAI is integrated into a solution, all the authentication can be done using secure encrypted channels, making it even harder for hackers to crack.

CHAPTER 11

THE BOTTOM LINE

"Security must begin at the top of an organization. It is a leadership issue, and the chief executive must set the example."

~ Unknown, heard at a security conference

Here's a fact that most CEOs and board members do not want to hear: your network is one mouse click away from a security breach. There is no silver bullet, one-size-fits-all solution to stop that click. Typically, what dictates the appropriate security within an organization is the value of the data, the attacker profile, the budget, the in-house technical expertise, and upper management's desire to manage the risk.

Often when technology is discussed, it becomes confusing to business owners. There are times when even I get glassy-eyed, and I live and breathe this stuff every day. You can greatly alleviate much of the confusion if you have an idea as to what you want to do. Think outside the box and focus on the problem you want solved. Finding the technology is the easy part.

To the IT managers, CISO and techies, start understanding how the business side of the business thinks, manages, and monitors success. They control the purse strings and if you need funds, you better start speaking their language. If anyone ever tells you that security does not have a quantifiable ROI, well, in my opinion, they don't understand business. Find someone who does.

The additional takeaways I hope you seize upon are:

- Certificates are not better than Passwords, or vice versa. They each have pros and cons.

- Encryption keys are nothing more than glorified passwords. They are just a string of zeros and ones.

- Even the best security, from a theoretical perspective, can be undermined by the *Human Element*.

- The more complex a system becomes, the greater the likelihood of a security breach.

- Categorize and segregate data, and then match the technology with the security requirements.

- Passwords are secure when password management is also secure.

Every size company, organization, and agency can affordably implement multi-factor authentication. Smartcard technology is no longer just for government and Fortune 500 companies. Today, you can customize the functionality of the ID badge like you customize your smartphone: simply add a new app.

President Obama's Cybersecurity National Action Plan reported on February 9, 2016 states:

> "**Empower Americans to secure their online accounts** by moving beyond just passwords and adding an extra layer of security. By judiciously combining a strong password with additional factors, such as a fingerprint or a single use code delivered in a text message, Americans can make their accounts even more secure. This focus on **multi-factor authentication** will be central to a new **National Cybersecurity Awareness Campaign** launched by the **National Cyber Security Alliance** designed to arm consumers with simple and actionable information to protect themselves in an increasingly digital world."

PAI makes passwords secure. By removing the employee from the role of password manager, cybersecurity's weakest link is eliminated.

ABOUT THE AUTHOR

Dovell Bonnett – "The Password Guy"

Dovell Bonnett has been creating computer security solutions for over 20 years. His passionate belief that technology should work for humans, and not the other way around, has lead him to create innovative solutions that protect businesses from cyber-attacks, free individual computer users from cumbersome security policies, and put IT administrators back in control of their networks.

He has spent most of his career designing solutions to solve business security needs, incorporating multiple applications onto single credentials using both contact and contactless smartcards. The most famous example of his work is the ID badge currently used by all Microsoft employees.

Back in 2000, Dovell was contacted by Indala (a division of Motorola) as a consultant to help them solve a security problem for one of their largest customers. The customer had just experienced a major cyber breach and the hacker had stolen important source code. The requirement was to create a single employee ID badge that would allow the employee secure authorized access into buildings and secure authorized access into computer networks.

After he explained to Indala how simple that would be, they immediately made Dovell their director of smartcard development. The customer turned out to be Microsoft and the project was the first time physical and logical access had been combined on a single corporate ID badge.

When the Indala division was sold by Motorola, the outgoing president told the new CEO he could get rid of all the upper management except Dovell because, "He is your visionary that will take you out five to ten years into the future." Dovell offered his new company the vision that businesses have two front doors: the physical and the virtual, opening up a whole new market potential. Unfortunately, the new CEO pushed back, saying, "Dovell, you don't understand our business. We make doors go 'beep.'" That eventually led Dovell to exit the corporate world so he could manifest his vision.

In 2005, he founded Access Smart LLC to provide logical access control solutions to businesses. His premiere product, Power LogOn, is a multi-factor authentication enterprise password manager used by corporations, hospitals, educational institutions, police departments, government agencies, and more.

Dovell has held positions at National Semiconductor, Siemens (Infineon), Certicom, Motorola, and HID. In addition to his involvement with Public Key Infrastructure (PKI) and Elliptic Curve Cryptography, he has also held a Top Secret security clearance with the United States Navy while working on communications for nuclear submarines at GTE Systems.

Dovell has contributed to numerous papers for the Smart Card Alliance organization; magazines, including *Card Manufacturing Magazine*; and is the author of two books, *Online Identity Theft Protection for Dummies®* and *Making Passwords Secure: How to Fix the Weakest Link in Cybersecurity*. Dovell is a frequent speaker and sought-after consultant on the topic of passwords, cybersecurity, and building secure, affordable and appropriate computer authentication infrastructures especially PAIs.

He can be contacted at:

Dovell Bonnett
Founder and CEO, Access Smart LLC
(949) 218-8754
Dovell@Access-Smart.com
www.Access-Smart.com

RESOURCES

Access Smart, LLC
https://www.access-smart.com

National Cyber Security Alliance
http://www.nationalsecurityalliance.net/

StaySafeOnline.org
https://staysafeonline.org/

InformationWeek Dark Reader
http://www.darkreading.com

PCI Security Standards Council
https://www.pcisecuritystandards.org/

CardLogix
http://www.cardlogix.com/

CardWerk
http://www.cardwerk.com/

BIBLIOGRAPHY

Aaron, Raymond, and Sue Lacher. *Double Your Income Doing What You Love: Raymond Aaron's Guide to Power Mentoring.* Hoboken, NJ: John Wiley & Sons, 2008.

Abraham, Jay. *The Sticking Point Solution: 9 Ways to Move Your Business from Stagnation to Stunning Growth in Tough Economic times.* New York: Vanguard Press, 2009.

Absolute. "The Cost of a Data Breach: Healthcare Settlements Involving Lost or Stolen Devices." *Engineering Information Security*, 2015, 461-516. doi:10.1002/9781119104728.ch09.

Agre, Philip, and Marc Rotenberg. *Technology and Privacy: The New Landscape.* Cambridge, MA: MIT Press, 1997.

Allen, Catherine A., William J. Barr, and Ron Schultz. *Smart Cards: Seizing Strategic Business Opportunities.* Chicago: Irwin Professional Pub., 1997.

Andress, Jason, Steve Winterfeld, and Russ Rogers. *Cyber Warfare: Techniques, Tactics and Tools for Security Practitioners.* Amsterdam: Syngress/Elsevier, 2011.

ANSI. *The Financial Impact of Breached Protected Health Information.* Report. 2012. http://webstore.ansi.org/phi/.

BeyondTrust. *6 Critical Capabilities of Password Management*. Report. October 28, 2015. https://www.beyondtrust.com/wp-content/uploads/wp-six-critical-capabilities-of-password-management.pdf.

Black, Uyless D. *Internet Security Protocols: Protecting IP Traffic*. Upper Saddle River, NJ: Prentice Hall PRT, 2000.

Bonnett, Dovell. "Chip Card's Business Case Requires PC Modeling." *Card Manufacturing*, September/October 1998.

Bonnett, Dovell. *Online Identity Theft Protection for Dummies*. Hoboken, NJ: Wiley Publishing, 2007.

Bouchard, Jim. *Think Like a Black Belt*. San Chi Publishing, 2010.

Bouchard, Jim. "Think Like A Black Belt: The Blog!" Think Like A Black Belt The Blog. Accessed February 02, 2014. http://thinklikeablackbelt.org/.

Boulton, Richard, Barry Libert, and Steve M. Samek. *Cracking the Value Code: How Successful Businesses Are Creating Wealth in the New Economy*. New York: HarperBusiness, 2000.

Bowers, Brent, and Carl J. Schramm. *If at First You Don't Succeed--: The Eight Patterns of Highly Effective Entrepreneurs*. New York: Currency/Doubleday, 2006.

Brands, Stefan A. *Rethinking Public Key Infrastructures and Digital Certificates: Building in Privacy*. Cambridge, MA: MIT Press, 2000.

Bright, Peter. "RSA Finally Comes Clean: SecurID Is Compromised." Ars Technica. June 6, 2011. http://arstechnica.com/security/2011/06/rsa-finally-comes-clean-securid-is-compromised/.

Brin, David. *The Transparent Society*. New York: Basic Books, 1998.

Burg, Bob, and John David. Mann. *Go-givers Sell More*. New York: Portfolio, 2010.

Canfield, Jack, and Janet Switzer. *The Success Principles: How to Get from Where You Are to Where You Want to Be.* New York: Harper Resource Book, 2005.

Carr, Jeffrey, and Lewis Shepherd. *Inside Cyber Warfare.* Sebastopol, CA: O'Reilly Media, 2010.

Carroll, John M. *Computer Security.* Los Angeles: Security World Pub., 1977.

Cavalancia, Nick. "6 Critical Capabilities of Password Management." *6 Critical Capabilities of Password Management.* https://www. beyondtrust.com/wp-content/uploads/wp-six-critical-capabilities-of-password-management.pdf.

Chen, Zhiqun. *Java Card Technology for Smart Cards: Architecture and Programmer's Guide.* Boston: Addison-Wesley, 2000.

Chickowski, Ericka. "The Secret Life Of Stolen Credentials." *DarkReading* (blog), February 18, 2016. http://www. darkreading.com/cloud/the-secret-life-of-stolen-credentials/d/d-id/1324366?utm_content=29125255&utm_medium=social&utm_source=linkedin.

Cohan, Peter E. *Great Demo!: How to Create and Execute Stunning Software Demonstrations.* New York: IUniverse, 2005.

Cunningham, Keith J. *The Ultimate Blueprint for an Insanely Successful Business.* Austin, TX: Keys to the Vault, 2011.

Cunningham, Keith J. *The Ultimate Blueprint for an Insanely Successful Business.* Austin, TX: Keys to the Vault, 2011.

"Customer Letter - Apple." *Apple* (blog), February 16, 2016. http://www. apple.com/customer-letter/.

De Clercq, Jan. "Smart Cards." Technet.microsoft.com. https://technet. microsoft.com/en-us/library/dd277362.aspx.

Dell Software. "Anatomy of a Cyber-attack." *Software.dell.com*, June 2013, 136. http://software.dell.com/documents/anatomy-of-a-cyber-attack-ebook-24640.pdf.

Deutsch, Debbie, and Beth Cohen. "Public Key Infrastructure: Invisibly Protecting Your Digital Assets." Enterprisenetworkingplanet.com. June 13, 2003. http://www.enterprisenetworkingplanet.com/netsecur/article.php/2223381/Public-Key-Infrastructure-Invisibly-Protecting-Your-Digital-Assets.htm.

Direct Tech. "Data & Business IT Asset Protection for SMBs." Directechca.com. November 2015. http://www.directechca.com/wp-content/uploads/2015/11/White-Paper-SMBs_WEB.pdf?e9eb59.

Donaldson, Scott E., Stanley G. Siegel, Chris K. Williams, and Abdul Aslam. *Enterprise Cybersecurity: How to Build a Successful Cyberdefense Program against Advanced Threats*. New York: Apress, 2015.

Doyle, Peter. *Value-based Marketing: Marketing Strategies for Corporate Growth and Shareholder Value*. Chichester: Wiley, 2000.

Dreifus, Henry, and J. Thomas. Monk. *Smart Cards: A Guide to Building and Managing Smart Card Applications*. New York: Wiley, 1998.

Drew, Grady N. *Using SET for Secure Electronic Commerce*. Upper Saddle River, NJ: Prentice Hall PTR, 1999.

Emord, Jonathan W. *Freedom, Technology, and the First Amendment*. San Francisco, CA: Pacific Research Institute for Public Policy, 1991.

Etzioni, Amitai. *The Limits of Privacy*. New York: Basic Books, 1999.

Evans, Donald L., Phillip J. Bond, and Arden L. Bement, Jr. *Standards for Security Categorization of Federal Information and Information Systems*. Gaithersburg, MD: Computer Security Division, Information Technology Laboratory, National Institute of Standards and Technology, 2003. http://csrc.nist.gov/publications/fips/ fips199/FIPS-PUB-199-final.pdf.

Federal Bureau of Investigation. "Ransomware on the Rise." FBI.gov. January 20, 2015. https://www.fbi.gov/news/stories/2015/january/ ransomware-on-the-rise/ransomware-on-the-rise.

Federal News Radio. "White House Cyber Czar's Goal: 'Kill the Password Dead'" Federalnewsradio.com. June 18, 2014. http://federalnewsradio.com/technology/2014/06/ white-house-cyber-czars-goal-kill-the-password-dead/.

Forrester, Merritt Maxim,, Jennie Duong, Alexander Spiliotes, and Peggy Peggy. "Benchmark Your Employee Password Policies And Practices." Forrester.com. September 9, 2015. https://www.forrester.com/ report/Benchmark+Your+Employee+Password+Policies+And+Prac tices/-/E-RES122799.

Foster, Mike. *The Secure CEO: How to Protect Your Computer Systems, Your Company, and Your Job*. Wichita, KS, USA: Prime Concepts Group Pub., 2008.

Frank, Mari J. *Safeguard Your Identity: Protect Yourself with a Personal Private Audit*. Laguna Niguel, CA: Porpoise Press, 2005.

Friedman, Lawrence G., and Timothy R. Furey. *The Channel Advantage: Going to Market with Multiple Sales Channels to Reach More Customers, Sell More Products, Make More Profit*. Oxford: Butterworth Heinemann, 1999.

Gladwell, Malcolm. *The Tipping Point: How Little Things Can Make a Big Difference*. Boston: Little, Brown, 2000.

Goodin, Dan. "Scientists Crack RSA SecurID 800 Tokens, Steal Cryptographic Keys." Ars Technica. June 25, 2012. http://arstech-nica.com/security/2012/06/securid-crypto-attack-steals-keys/.

Greenberg, Andy. "Hack Brief: Password Manager LastPass Got Breached Hard." Wired.com. June 15, 2015. http://www.wired.com/2015/06/hack-brief-password-manager-lastpass-got-breached-hard/.

Guthery, Scott B., and Timothy M. Jurgensen. *Smart Card: Developer's Kit*. Indianapolis, IN: Macmillan Technical Pub., 1998.

Hagel, John, John Seely. Brown, and Lang Davison. *The Power of Pull: How Small Moves, Smartly Made, Can Set Big Things in Motion*. New York: Basic Books, 2010.

Hall, Grant. *Privacy Crisis: Identity Theft Prevention Plan and Guide to Anonymous Living*. Mesa, AZ: James Clark King, LLC, 2006.

Hanan, Mack, and Peter Karp. *Competing on Value*. New York, NY: AMACOM, 1991.

Hendry, Mike. *Smart Card Security and Applications*. Boston: Artech House, 2001.

Hewlett Packard Enterprise. "Internet of Things Research Study." *Internet of Things Research Study*, November 2015. doi:10.1109/jiot.2015.2462874.

Higgins, Kelly Jackson. "Digital Certificate Authority Hacked, Dozens Of Phony Digital Certificates Issued." Dark Reading. August 30, 2011. http://www.darkreading.com/attacks-breaches/digital-certificate-authority-hacked-dozens-of-phony-digital-certificates-issued/d/d-id/1136244.

Hodges, Andrew. *Alan Turing: The Enigma*. Princeton University Press., 2014.

Holtzman, David H. *Privacy Lost: How Technology Is Endangering Your Privacy*. San Francisco: Jossey-Bass, 2006.

Housley, Russ, and Tim Polk. *Planning for PKI: Best Practices Guide for Deploying Public Key Infrastructure*. New York: Wiley, 2001.

IBM. "IBM X-Force Threat Intelligence Report 2016." *IBM Security*, February 2016. doi:10.1515/9781400857999.8.

Intel Security. "Threat Report." *McAfee Labs*, November 2014. http://www.mcafee.com/us/resources/reports/rp-quarterly-threat-q3-2014.pdf.

Intel Security. "Threats Predictions." *McAfee Labs*, 2015. doi:10.5040/9781472596857.ch-011.

Isaacson, Walter. *The Innovators: How a Group of Hackers, Geniuses, and Geeks Created the Digital Revolution.*

Jurgensen, Timothy M., and Scott B. Guthery. *Smart Cards: The Developer's Toolkit*. Upper Saddle River, NJ: Prentice Hall, 2002.

Kaplan, Jack M. *Smart Cards: The Global Information Passport*. London: International Thomas Computer Press, 1996.

Kaplan, Steve. *Bag the Elephant!: How to Win & Keep Big Customers*. Austin, TX: Bard Press, 2005.

Kent, Eileen. "The Federal Sales Sherpa." The Federal Sales Sherpa. Accessed May 2, 2014. http://federalsalessherpa.com/.

Kirkham, Elyssa. "Visa and MasterCard Switching to EMV Smart Cards by 2015 | GOBankingRates." GOBankingRates. February 10, 2014. http://www.gobankingrates.com/credit-cards/mastercard-visa-emv-smartcard-switch-2015/.

Kiyosaki, Robert T., and Sharon L. Lechter. *Rich Dad Poor Dad: What The Rich Teach Their Kids About Money - That The Poor And Middle Class Do Not!* Plata Publishing; 2nd Edition, 2011.

Krutz, Ronald L., and Russell Dean Vines. *Security Prep Guide*. Indianapolis, IN: Wiley, 2003.

Lendrum, Tony. *The Strategic Partnering Handbook: The Practitioners' Guide to Partnerships and Alliances.* Sydney: McGraw-Hill, 2003.

Levison, Ladar. "Lavabit." Lavabit. May 20, 2014. http://lavabit.com/.

Levy, Steven. *Crypto: How the Code Rebels Beat the Government, Saving Privacy in the Digital Age.* New York: Viking, 2001.

Loberg, Kristin. *Identity Theft: How to Protect Your Name, Your Credit and Your Vital Information-- and What to Do When Someone Hijacks Any of These.* Los Angeles, CA: Silver Lake Pub., 2004.

Marcum, David, Steven Smith, and Mahan Khalsa. *BusinessThink: Rules for Getting It Right--now, and No Matter What!* New York: Wiley, 2002.

May, Johnny R. *Johnny May's Guide to Preventing Identity Theft: How Criminals Steal Your Personal Information, How to Prevent It, and What to Do If You Become a Victim.* Bloomfield Hills, MI?: Security Resources Unlimited, 2004.

McCarthy, Linda. *IT Security: Risking the Corporation.* Upper Saddle River, NJ: Prentice Hall, 2002.

McCarthy, Mary Pat., Stuart Campbell, and Rob Brownstein. *Security Transformation: Digital Defense Strategies to Protect Your Company's Reputation and Market Share.* New York: McGraw-Hill, 2001.

Mell, Peter, and Timothy Grance. "The NIST Definition of Cloud Computing - Special Publication 800-145." *NIST SP 800-145, The NIST Definition of Cloud Computing*, September 2011. http://nvlpubs.nist.gov/nistpubs/Legacy/SP/nistspecialpublication800-145.pdf.

Merkow, Mark S., and Jim Breithaupt. *The Complete Guide to Internet Security.* New York: AMACOM, 2000.

Merkow, Mark S., Jim Breithaupt, and Ken L. Wheeler. *Building SET Applications for Secure Transactions*. New York: Wiley, 1998.

Mitnick, Kevin D., and William L. Simon. *The Art of Deception: Controlling the Human Element of Security*. Indianapolis, IN: Wiley Pub., 2002.

Mitnick, Kevin D., and William L. Simon. *Ghost in the Wires: My Adventures as the World's Most Wanted Hacker*. New York: Little, Brown and Company, 2011.

Nichols, Shaun. "Hackers Steal Files on 4 Million US Govt Workers." Www.theregister.co.uk. June 5, 2015. http://www.theregister.co.uk/2015/06/05/opm_data_breach/.

The Ohio State University. "A JOURNAL OF LAW AND POLICY FOR THE INFORMATION SOCIETY." I/S: A Journal of Law and Policy for the Information Society. Accessed February 02, 2016. http://www.is-journal.org/.

Olson, Parmy. *We Are Anonymous: Inside the Hacker World of Lulzsec, Anonymous, and the Global Cyber Insurgency*. New York: Little, Brown and, 2012.

O'reilly, Patrick D., Gregory A. Witte, and Larry Feldman. "Computer Security Division 2014 Annual Report." August 2015. doi:10.6028/nist.sp.800-176.

"Password." Dictionary.com. http://dictionary.reference.com/.

Ponemon Institute. "2015 Cost of Failed Trust Report." Venafi.com. 2015. https://www.venafi.com/offers/trust-established-by-keys-and-certificates-is-in-jeopardy.

Ponemon Institute LLC. "2015 Cost of Data Breach Study:." May 2015. http://www-01.ibm.com/common/ssi/cgi-bin/ssialias?subtype=WH&infotype=SA&htmlfid=SEW03053W-WEN&attachment=SEW03053WWEN.PDF.

Poulsen, Kevin. *Kingpin: How One Hacker Took over the Billion-dollar Cybercrime Underground*. New York: Crown Publishers, 2011.

"Public Law 108-197 108th Congress." *Federal Information Security Management Act (FISMA) of 2002, Public Law 107-347*, December 17, 2002. doi:10.1037/e310052005-001.

Qualman, Erik. *Socialnomics: How Social Media Transforms the Way We Live and Do Business*. Hoboken, NJ: Wiley, 2009.

Rackham, Neil, Lawrence G. Friedman, and Richard Ruff. *Getting Partnering Right: How Market Leaders Are Creating Long-term Competitive Advantage*. New York: McGraw-Hill, 1996.

The Radicati Group, Inc. "APT Protection - Market Quadrant, 2015." Radicati.com. Accessed March 04, 2016. http://www.radicati.com/?p=13077.

Rankl, Wolfgang, and Wolfgang Effing. *Smart Card Handbook*. Chichester: Wiley, 2003.

Raytheon and Websense. "Cybersecurity and Data Theft Prevention: What Every Board of Directors Should Know About Managing Risk in Their Organization." *A High Level Primer for Every Member of the Board*, August 26, 2015. http://f6ce14d4647f05e937f4-4d6ab-ce208e5e17c2085b466b98c2083.r3.cf1.rackcdn.com/five-key-tenets-cybersecurity-oversight-pdf-1-w-1889.pdf.

Raytheon and Websense Security Labs, |. "2016 Security Predictions." *An Annual Report by Raytheon & Websence Security Labs*, December 02, 2015. http://www.e92plus.com/Files/report-2016-cybersecurity-pre-dictions-en.pdf.

Rolnicki, Kenneth. *Managing Channels of Distribution*. New York: AMACOM, 1998.

Rosen, Jeffrey. *The Unwanted Gaze: The Destruction of Privacy in America*. New York: Random House, 2000.

Rosso, John. *Prospect the Sandler Way*. Sandler Systems, 2014.

Scambray, Joel, Stuart McClure, and George Kurtz. *Hacking Exposed: Network Security Secrets & Solutions*. Berkeley, CA: Osborne/ McGraw-Hill, 2001.

Scarfone, Karen, and Murugiah Souppaya. "Guide to Enterprise Password Management (Draft)." *NIST SP 800-118, Guide to Enterprise Password Management (DRAFT)*, April 2009. http://csrc.nist.gov/ publications/drafts/800-118/draft-sp800-118.pdf.

Schneier, Bruce. *Applied Cryptography: Protocols, Algorithms, and Source Code in C Edition 20th Anniversary Edition*. Indianapolis, IN: Wiley, 2015.

Schneier, Bruce. *Secrets and Lies: Digital Security in a Networked World*. New York: John Wiley, 2000.

Sinek, Simon. *Start with Why: How Great Leaders Inspire Everyone to Take Action*. New York: Portfolio, 2009.

Singer, P. W. *Cybersecurity and Cyberwar: What Everyone Needs to Know*. Oxford: Oxford University Press, 2014.

"STATEMENT OF GENERAL KEITH B. ALEXANDER COMMANDER UNITED STATES CYBER COMMAND BEFORE THE SENATE COMMITTEE ON ARMED SERVICES." *Airforcemag.com*, March 24, 2012. http://www.airforce-mag.com/SiteCollectionDocuments/Reports/2012/March2012/Day28/032812alexander.pdf.

Stephenson, Neal. *Cryptonomicon*. New York: Avon Press, 1999.

Stephenson, Peter. *Investigating Computer-related Crime*. Boca Raton, Fla: CRC Press, 2000.

Stern, Louis W., and Adel I. Ansary. *Marketing Channels, Seventh Edition*. Englewood Cliffs, NJ: Prentice-Hall, 2014.

Sullivan, Bob. *Your Evil Twin: Behind the Identity Theft Epidemic.* Hoboken, NJ: John Wiley & Sons, 2004.

Sullivan, Nick. "The Results of the CloudFlare Challenge." CloudFlare. April 11, 2014. Accessed March 05, 2016. https://blog.cloudflare.com/the-results-of-the-cloudflare-challenge/.

Sunzi, and Gerald A. Michaelson. *Sun Tzu: The Art of War for Managers: 50 Strategic Rules.* Avon, MA: Adams Media, 2001.

Sunzi, and Samuel B. Griffith. *The Art of War.* London: Oxford University Press, 1971.

Symantec. "Beginner's Guide to SSL Certificates." June 10, 2013. doi:10.1007/978-1-4419-8760-0.

Symantec. "Security Response Publications." Internet Security Threat Report 2015. Accessed March 04, 2016. http://www.symantec.com/security_response/publications/threatreport.jsp?cid=70150000000diToAAI&om_sem_cid=biz_sem_273692754025047%7Cpcrid%7C9711531381%7Cp-mt%7Cp%7Cplc%7C%7Bplacement%7D%7Cpdv%7Cc.

TeamsID. "Announcing Our Worst Passwords of 2015 | TeamsID." TeamsID.com. January 19, 2016. https://www.teamsid.com/worst-passwords-2015/.

Thompson, Harvey. *The Customer-centered Enterprise: How IBM and Other World-class Companies Achieve Extraordinary Results by Putting Customers First.* New York: McGraw-Hill, 2000.

Tom Gjelter. *Southern California Public Radio - 89.3 KPCC.* Report. October 16, 2013. http://www.scpr.org/news/2013/10/16/39843/are-we-moving-to-a-world-with-more-online-surveill/.

Underhill, Paco. *Why We Buy: The Science of Shopping.* New York: Simon & Schuster, 1999.

United States of America. NIST. Security Management & Assurance.
NIST Computer Security Division. By PATRICK O'REILLY. August
2015. http://nvlpubs.nist.gov/nistpubs/SpecialPublications/NIST.
SP.800-176.pdf.

U.S. Department of Homeland Security. "Homeland Security Presidential
Directive-12: Policies for a Common Identification Standard for
Federal Employees and Contractors." DHS.gov. August 27, 2004.
https://www.dhs.gov/homeland-security-presidential-directive-12.

U.S. Office of Management and Budget. "CIRCULAR NO. A-130
Revised." WhiteHouse.gov. November 28, 2000. https://www.
whitehouse.gov/omb/circulars_a130_a130trans4/.

Verisign. "2016 Cyberthreats and Trends Report." 2016 Cyberthreats
and Trends Report. 2016. https://www.verisign.com/en_US/forms/
reportcyberthreatstrends.xhtml.

VERIZON ENTERPRISE SOLUTIONS. "2015 Data Breach
Investigations Report." Verizonenterprise.com. April 2015. http://
www.verizonenterprise.com/DBIR/2015/?utm_source=pr&utm_
medium=pr&utm_campaign=dbir2015.

Walker, Jeff. "Product Launch Formula." Jeff Walker. Accessed 2013.
http://jeffwalker.com/.

Websense Security Labs. "2015 Threat Report Download." 2015 Threat
Report Download. April 8, 2015. http://www.websense.com/con-
tent/websense-2015-threat-report.aspx.

White House. "FACT SHEET: Cybersecurity National Action
Plan." The White House. February 09, 2016. https://
www.whitehouse.gov/the-press-office/2016/02/09/
fact-sheet-cybersecurity-national-action-plan.

Wilson, Chuck. *Get Smart: The Emergence of Smart Cards in the United
States and Their Pivotal Role in Internet Commerce: A Comprehensive
Review.* Richardson, TX: Mullaney Pub. Group, 2001.

Winkler, Ira. *Corporate Espionage: What It Is, Why It Is Happening in Your Company, What You Must Do about It*. Rocklin, CA: Prima Pub., 1997.

Yoffie, David B., and Mary Kwak. *Judo Strategy: Turning Your Competitors' Strength to Your Advantage*. Boston, MA: Harvard Business School Press, 2001.

Zaltman, Gerald. *How Customers Think: Essential Insights into the Mind of the Market*. Boston, MA: Harvard Business School Press, 2003.

Zoreda, José Luis., and José Manuel. Otón. *Smart Cards*. Boston: Artech House, 1994.

A CLOSING NOTE FROM ME

As you probably can tell, I love passwords and believe through proper management they are secure. One of the best ways to start is by reviewing Chapter 10: "Implementing a Multi-Factor Password Authentication Infrastructure" again. If you are interested in learning more about how a PAI can work in your company, agency or small business, then I have a free gift for you.

The one common denominator when it comes to all computer networks is that there is no one common denominator. I am offering you a free, one-hour consultation where you can ask me anything about secure authentication, smartcards, or combining physical and cyber access control. If I don't know the answer, I will point you to the people or companies who will.

All you have to do is navigate over to http://www.MakingPasswordsSecure.com/contact-us/, Select "**Consultation**", type "**My free 1hr session**" in the email subject line, and fill in your contact information. Let me know your preferred day and time you would like to talk. Please include a couple of alternative days and times to help coordinate both our schedules.

Contact me now and you could have a PAI system up and running within days. Really!

Have a look at https://www.access-smart.com/power-logon/ if you want to research a PAI solution that includes <u>everything</u> to start a test pilot.

Made in the USA
Middletown, DE
23 January 2024

48248393R00095